Welsh
NAMES

Welsh
NAMES

D. Geraint Lewis

GEDDES & GROSSET

Dedication

Dedicated to the memory of the good people of Ynys-y-bŵl,
so many of whose names inhabit these pages.

First published 2001 by Geddes & Grosset, an imprint of
Children's Leisure Products Limited, David Dale House,
New Lanark, ML11 9DJ, Scotland

© 2001 D. Geraint Lewis

ISBN 1 84205 073 7

Printed and bound in Europe

Contents

Foreword

This book attempts three things:
1 a selection of Welsh first names from Welsh history and romance
2 a selection of Welsh surnames and their derivations
3 a list of village nicknames collected originally by the author's grand-father.

   Lists of children's names can be found in *Enwau Cymraeg i Blant/ Welsh Names for Children* by Heini Gruffudd (published by Y Lolfa, Talybont) and *Welsh Names for Your Children* by Meic Stephens (published by Ashley Drake Publishing, Cardiff). A standard work on early Welsh names is A *Welsh Classical Dictionary: People in History and Legend up to about AD 1000* by Peter C. Bartrum (published by the National Library of Wales, Aberystwyth). The other standard work I have drawn on is *Welsh Surnames* by T J Morgan and Prys Morgan (published by the University of Wales Press, Cardiff).

Introduction

I was brought up in a south Wales mining village. My grandfather's mother-tongue was Welsh and both my parents were able to speak Welsh but I had to learn it.

This is a situation that many adults of my generation would recognise. What it has taken me far longer to appreciate is the manner in which my parents' generation passed on their sense of identity in the names they gave to us, their children. My sister is called Rhiannon and in the same street lived Gwyddfid, Gwlithyn, Glynis, Glyndwr, Teifi, Llywela and Teifion. Contemporaries at chapel were called Alwyn, Egryn, Tecwyn, Llinos and Eirianwen. There were also Eurof, Idwal, Buddug, Tegwen, Mairwen, Meirwyn, and Myrdeg. Uncle Elwyn, Auntie Gwladus, and my cousins Gurwyn and Aelonwy lived in the village.

Some years later, in college, I was required to look at the names used by the formal court poets of Wales in their compositions as standards of beauty, valour, treachery etc. Over the centuries, the bardic tutors had accumulated an oral encyclopaedia of such names collected in threes under a particular attribute, thus:

- 'The Three Generous Men of the Isle of Britain' were Nudd, son of Senyllt, Mordaf, son of Serwan, and Rhydderch, son of Tudwal Tudglyd.
- 'The Three Fair Maidens of the Isle of Britain' were Creirwy, daughter of Ceridwen, Arianrhod, daughter of Dôn, and Gwen, daughter of Cywryd, son of Crydon.

These *trioedd* or 'triads' eventually came to be set down, and one of the later triads summarises the nature of bardic duty, which was to preserve the 'Three Memories of the Isle of Britain'. One of these memories entailed the preservation of the Welsh language and the art of poetic composition. Another was to retain for posterity the history of the notable acts of kings and princes. The third memory was that of the genealogies of descent of the Welsh nobility.

Introduction

Two of these 'memories' required an encyclopaedic knowledge of Welsh names – the names of the kings and princes and heroes who accomplished the notable acts (in both fact and fiction) which made up the history of Wales and the names that constituted the pedigrees of the Welsh nobility.

This bardic tradition takes us back to the emergence of the Welsh language and to names such as Aneirin and Taliesin in the sixth century when there was no such entity as Wales. However, we cannot move in modern Wales without being reminded of an even earlier inheritance which preceded the Welsh language. Consider the number of place names and parishes in Wales that begin with *Llan* (the church of), the vast majority of which (though not all) are then followed by the name of a saint. A significant number of these names are those of Celtic saints who travelled freely between what we now call Ireland, Wales, northern England/southern Scotland, Devon and Cornwall and Brittany. During the fourth and fifth centuries when these travels took place, the British mother tongue of Welsh, Cornish and Breton was the vernacular tongue, while Latin was the language of the church. It is worth noting that the Celtic monastic tradition had an honourable place for women, and a number of female saints are recorded and commemorated in these place names, names such as Non and Ffraid, while Dewi, Teilo, Illtud and Padarn are names that resonate to this day.

I see in the practice of giving my generation of non-Welsh-speaking children picturesque and historic Welsh names a vestige of that duty to preserve the noble deeds and histories that have reached down the centuries. These names form part of the nation's memory of a heritage which extends beyond the emergence of the Welsh language in the sixth century back through the early centuries of the British Christian Age to the prehistoric world of Celtic myth.

The renaissance of Welsh in the latter part of the twentieth century has seen the development and growth of this practice. And it continues to flourish, as I was pleasantly reminded when checking this list of names with the names of members of the joint youth choir of Carmarthenshire, Pembrokeshire and Ceredigion.

Surnames were introduced into Wales as a result of increasing anglicisation following the Acts of Union (1536, 1548). Welsh tradition identified a person from the father's name *Dafydd ap* (son of) *Gwilym;* before a vowel the *ap* became *ab,* e.g. *Dafydd ab Owain.* The name of the father, of course, changed from generation to generation and there remained no identifiable family name which was a requirement of the English legal system. One way of creating surnames was to add the possessive 's to forenames, thus William(s), and Evans (from Ifan).

However, remnants of the older Welsh system are still to be found in such names as Bowen (ab Owen), Powell (ap Hywel), Pritchard (ap Rhisiart), Price (ap Rhys). Moreover, the practice of using the 'ap' system continues to this day, as any examination of a current telephone directory will demonstrate.

Another means of distinguishing between two people sharing the same forename, would be to ascribe an adjective to one of them. In English, this would precede the noun, e.g. 'Black Jack'. In Welsh, the adjective would follow the noun, e.g. *Dafydd Llwyd* (grey [haired] Dafydd) and a number of such adjectives have been turned into anglicised surnames, e.g. Vaughan from *fychan* (small or junior), Lloyd from *llwyd* (grey), Gough from *coch* (red).

Another means of identifying a person is to add a place of origin to the forename. In English this leads to 'John of Gaunt'. However, the 'of' equivalent is not necessary in Welsh; *Siôn Mawddach* equates to 'Sion of Mawddach'. Such place names were popular and some were eventually to turn into surnames.

A variation on this is the long-standing method in rural areas of relating a person to his or her farm or smallholding, thus distinguishing between *Dewi Ty'n Beili* and *Dewi Rhandir Uchaf* or referring to *Mair Tynllwyn* as opposed to *Mair Brynchwyth*. This method treats both sexes equally, and though long-standing and in active use, is vernacular and informal.

As the spiral of change uncoils, and Wales has become more urbanised, it has become fashionable to drop the anglicised surname and to use both a person's forenames, with the second name taking on the force of a surname, e.g. Dafydd Iwan, Angharad Mair, Hywel Gwynfryn, in what might be seen as a non-sexist reversion to the old Welsh way of naming.

In bardic circles, when there were more than one John Jones or William Williams etc., the poet would adopt a bardic name which would be more familiar to people than his baptismal names, thus *Caledfryn, Crwys, Nantlais* and *Creuddynfab* were all poets originally named William Williams.

There is one sport of this process for which the heavily populated valleys of the south Wales coal field became well known, but was as true of the quarrying villages of the north, namely the nickname. For example, of the sixteen houses in the street where I was born, all but two of the men worked in the pit. Those that didn't might well be known by their occupation – Thomas the Milk, James the Grocer,

Introduction

Jones the Ironmonger. However, with so many John Joneses, William Williamses and Evan Evanses all crowded into a single workplace, another means of identification was required. Sometimes this was the place name mentioned above but, more famously, underground where all men were black, it became the humorous nickname. John Evans, the father of our next-door neighbours, was known after his (formidable) wife as Shoni Gladys. Thomas Jones, who played the piano in the silent cinema, was Tommy Onetune, and his son was Billy Onetune, while the owner of the local sweet shop was Dai Minty.

I have included a list of the nicknames of one village, recalled in the 1950s by my grandfather Jonathan Thomas, a carpenter, and his friend, Johnny Morgan, a leader of the miners in his day and author of *A Village Workers' Council* (1951). My grandfather was born in Cardiganshire in 1875 and moved as a lad to Ynys-y-bŵl, the new 'Klondike' where he became a carpenter and undertaker. He died in 1957. These names were written down by my Auntie Sal, who made tea for the old gentlemen and interpreted for them as they were both, by that time, deaf.

The first coal produced by the Lady Windsor Colliery at Ynys-y-bŵl appeared in 1886, so this list of names goes back to the beginning of large-scale coal production in the village.

Prior to the discovery of coal, there was no village as such and a vivid picture of those rural times has been painted in *The History of Llanwonno*, the Welsh original of which is considered a little classic of its kind. The unquestionable 'war' that raged between the coal owners and the miners has been the subject of many south Wales histories and *A Village Workers' Council* is very much the diary of a war correspondent.

But in the nicknames recorded here are the vestiges of another community – the Welsh language community reflected in a book of short stories based on Ynys-y-bŵl, *Straeon y Gilfach Ddu* (The Stories of Gilfach Ddu), which reflects a society in which music, poetry, chapel and a closely shared community life went hand in hand with the hardship of working underground. While accepting the rosy hue through which the village is viewed in these tales, there is no doubt that this was a facet of that early mining community, which has perhaps not received the attention it deserves.

The Lady Windsor Colliery closed in 1988 and where once stood the sprawl of buildings and the characteristic winding gear of a major colliery, there now lie green fields and reclaimed tips. The names collected here reflect the heyday of a century of mining history and a way of life that has gone the way of the colliery itself.

There are too many colliers who have testified to the value they placed on the camaraderie that existed underground to ignore this. But in setting out such a list of names in a somewhat light-hearted manner, I would not wish for a moment to detract from the sheer slog, danger, and appalling conditions in which these men worked many hundreds of feet underground.

The pit has disappeared. Only a tablet of stone remains to recall *arwyr glew erwau'r glo* (the brave heroes of the coalfields). But the names of these heroes, too, have their place in the memories of the history of the Isle of Britain, themselves now a fossilised remnant of a once mighty forest.

An A–Z of Welsh Names

m – a masculine name
f – a feminine name
* – a surname

A

Adda *m*
The Welsh for the Biblical Adam, the first man.

Adwen *f*
An early Celtic saint and daughter of BRYCHAN.

Aelwen *f*
A girl's name meaning 'fair-browed', from a combination of *ael* 'brow' and *wen* 'fair'.

Aelwyn, Aylwyn *m*
Masculine variants of AELWEN.

Aeres *f*
The Welsh for 'heiress'. Aeres Evans was an authoress and collector of Carmarthenshire folk tales.

Aeron *m*
The name of a river in Ceredigion as found in *Aberaeron*, the *on* end-ing suggesting the name of a Celtic god or goddess.

Aerona, Aeronwy *f*
Feminine variants of AERON. Aeronwy is the name Dylan Thomas gave his daughter.

Aeronwen *f*
A feminine combination of AERON with the ending *wen*, meaning 'fair', 'bright' or 'blessed'.

Aethwy *m*
A bardic name from *Porthaethwy* (Menai Bridge).

Afagddu *m*
The son of the sorceress CERIDWEN. He was so ugly that she decided to give him, in compensation, the gift of all knowledge. *The Tale of TALIESIN* tells how this was acquired instead by the poet Taliesin.

Afallach *m*
A legendary king of the British. It was to the island of *Afallach* that ARTHUR was taken following his wounding at the Battle of Camlan. It was to become the Isle of Avalon in English.

Afan *m*
A fifth-century Celtic saint and Glamorgan river name. Afan Ferddig was one of the 'red-speared' bards in the lists of the triads and a poet from the earliest period of Welsh poetry.

Afarwy *m*
A name from the early annals of Welsh history, where he is portrayed as friend of Julius Caesar, and one of the 'Three Dishonoured Men' for the aid he gave Caesar on his second invasion of Britain.

Alaw *f and m*
The Welsh name for a 'melody', and a river name in Anglesey poignantly associated with the death of BRANWEN. John Parry, *Bardd Alaw,* was a famous nineteenth-century harpist.

Alban *m*
The Welsh for Scotland, and the name of an early Christian saint martyred at Saint Albans in the fourth century. Gareth Alban Davies is a contemporary Welsh poet and former professor of Spanish.

Alcwyn *m*
The Welsh form of the English name Alcuin. Alcuin (735–804) was an English scholar and theologian, a friend and adviser to Charlemagne.

Aled *m*
A river name in the former Denbighshire adopted by Tudur Aled, the medieval poet. Aled Jones was a boy soprano who gained great popularity.

Alis *f*
Alis Rhonwen was the name of the Saxon Hengist's daughter, with whom King Gwrtheyrn fell in love. King Gwrtheyrn allowed Hengist land in the south of England and the poets referred to Saxons (*Saeson*) or the English as 'the children of Alis'. Alis derives from a contracted version of the Germanic name Adalheidis.

Allet, Allett *
Surnames derived from ALED.

Alun *m*
A legendary hero of the ancient kingdom of DYFED and river name in the former Flintshire, adopted as a bardic name by John Blackwell, the popular 19th-century poet. Alun Lewis was a poet and literary figure killed in the Second World War and 'Alun Mabon' is the title of a popular Welsh poem.

Alwen, Alwena *f*
From the River Alwen in Clwyd.

'Alwen Hoff' (Beloved Alwen) is the title of a popular Welsh song.

Alwyn *m*
A male version of ALWEN. There is an English version which could be a variant of Alvin. Alwyn D Rees was an influential editor and writer.

Alys *f*
A variant of ALIS.

Amaethon *m*
A Celtic god of agriculture and one of the children of the Celtic goddess Dôn.

Amanwy *m*
The bardic name of David GRIFFITHS, a school caretaker whose life became the subject of a film called *David*.

Amig *m*
From the Charlemagne cycle of tales; the knights, Amig and Amlyn, epitomised friendship unto death.

Amlyn *m see* AMIG.

Anatiamaros *m*
This is the name of the 'great spirit' who led his people in ancient Gaul, in the poem of the same name by T Gwynn Jones.

Andras *m*
As in *Llanandras*, the Welsh name for Presteigne; a variant of ANDREAS. Andras Millward is the author of contemporary fantasy/ science fiction Welsh books for young people.

Andreas *m*
The Welsh form of the Biblical Andrew, Jesus' first disciple.

Aneira *f*
A girl's name based on *eira* 'snow'.

Aneirin, Aneurin *m*
From the name of the sixth-century 'prince of poets', Aneirin, who composed in the area that today is Catterick in Yorkshire. Aneurin Bevan was a great reforming Labour politician.

Angharad *f*
A popular girl's name based on *cariad*, the Welsh word for 'love'. Angharad Tomos is an important contemporary Welsh novelist and writer of children's books and Angharad Mair is a television presenter and athlete.

Anna *f*
The fictitious cousin of the Virgin Mary, also the sister of ARTHUR in Welsh legend.

Annest, Anest *f*
The name of a daughter of a twelfth-century king of Gwynedd, and possibly a variant of NEST.

Anwen *f*
A girl's name based on *wen*, the feminine form of *gwyn* 'fair' or 'blessed'.

Anwyl, Annwyl m *
A forename and surname from the Welsh *annwyl* 'dear' or 'beloved'.

Ap, Ab
Means 'son of'. It derives from *mab*, the Welsh word for 'son' and corresponds to the Gaelic *mac*. The feminine equivalent is *ach* from *merch* meaning 'daughter of', e.g. *Marged ach Ifan*. However, it was rarely used and has not been adopted to create modern surnames. Ap DAFYDD, ap GWYNEDD, ap STEFFAN are examples of current surnames taken at random from a telephone directory.

Arawn m
A king of the Welsh underworld (*annwfn*). How a friendship developed between him and PWYLL, Prince of DYFED, is the subject of the first of the branches of the tales of the *Mabinogion*.

Arfon m
The region in north Wales, from *ar* 'opposite' and *Fôn* 'Môn', 'Anglesey'. Arfon Haines Davies is a television presenter.

Arial m
The Welsh for 'vigour'.

Arianrhod f
The Celtic moon-goddess and a daughter of Dôn famed for her beauty. The 'Milky Way' is known as *Caer Arianrhod* (The Fortress of Arianrhod) in Welsh.

Arianwen f
One of the saintly daughters of BRYCHAN, her name derives from *arian* 'silver' and *wen* 'white' or 'pure'. Arianwen Parry was a pioneering Welsh bookshop owner.

Arnallt m
The Welsh form of Arnold.

Aron m
The Welsh form of the Biblical Aaron, brother of Moses. Also a name from the early *Stanzas of the Graves*.

Arthur m
A rough and ready sixth-century leader of the Britons who acquired a court and all the trappings of an emperor by the time his tales were recounted on the continent in medieval times.

Arwel m
The Welsh for 'prominent'. Arwel Hughes was an important Welsh composer.

Arwen, Arwenna f
Femine forms of ARWYN.

Arwyn m
Welsh for 'fair' or 'handsome'.

Aures f
Either a variant of AERES or a similar name based on *aur* 'gold'.

Aurfryn m
A variant of EURFRYN based on *aur* 'gold' and *bryn* 'hill'.

Aurona *f*
A variant of EURON based on the same root *aur* 'gold'.

Auryn *m*
A variant of EURYN from *aur* 'gold'.

Awela *f*
A girl's name based on *awel* 'zephyr'.

Awen, Awena *f*
The Welsh for the 'muse'.

Awstin *m*
The Welsh form of (St) Augustine.

Aylwyn *m*
A variant of AELWYN.

B

Baglan *m*
A sixth-century Celtic saint and student of St Illtud, commemorated in the place name by Port Talbot.

Banadl *m*
An early king of Powys; also Welsh for the 'flowering broom'.

Barti *m*
A diminutive form of Bartholomew. The most famous Barti of them all was the pirate, Barti Ddu o Gasnewy Bach (Black Bart from Pembrokeshire).

Beca *f*
A diminutive form of REBECA. *Merched Beca* (the Daughters of [Re]beca) was the term used for those men of southwest Wales who, in the mid-nineteenth century, dressed up as women to attack and destroy the toll-gates.

Beddoes *
A surname from Bedo, a diminutive form of MAREDUDD.

Bedwyr *m*
One of the two faithful companions of the Welsh ARTHUR. Bedwyr became the Bedivere of medieval romance. Bedwyr Lewis Jones was a Welsh language scholar and popular broadcaster.

Begw *f*
A diminutive affectionate form of MEGAN. A name made popular by the work of Kate Roberts, the Welsh short-story writer.

Bellin, Belling *
Surnames from Belyn, a powerful military leader of the seventh century.

Bellis *
A surname from ab Elis. *See* ELIS.

Bendigeidfran *m*
The full form of the name BRÂN. The god/king of the second branch of the tales of the *Mabinogion* who waded the Irish Sea and made him-

self into a bridge which his army could cross.

Bennion, Benyon, Beynon *
Surnames from ab Ein(i)on. *See* EINION.

Berian *m*
As in the place name *Brynberian* in Pembrokeshire. Berian Price was a Welsh runner.

Berwen *f*
A feminine form of BERWYN.

Berwyn *m*
A mountain range in northeast Wales; also one of ARTHUR's knights.

Bethan *f*
A Welsh affectionate form of Beth (from Elisabeth); also a variant of Bechan, daughter of BRYCHAN. Bethan Gwanas is a contemporary novelist and short-story writer.

Beti, Betsan *f*
Diminutive forms of Elisabeth.

Beuno *m*
The sixth-century patron saint of Gwynedd 'who stood for sanity in the insanities of the world in which he found himself'.

Bevan *
A surname from ab IFAN, Bifan.

Blainey *
A surname from the Welsh *blaenau* 'uplands'.

Bleddyn *m*
From *blaidd* 'wolf', an epithet for heroes in medieval Welsh poetry. Bleddyn Williams was a famous rugby player and then sports commentator in his day.

Blethyn, Blethin, Blevin, Blythin *
Surnames from BLEDDYN.

Blodeuwedd *f*
'The fairest maid that man ever saw' who was created by Math and Gwydion as a wife for Lleu from the flowers of the oak, the broom and the meadowsweet. But she possessed no human heart. Her story is told in the third branch of the tales of the *Mabinogion*.

Blodwen *f*
From *blodau* 'flowers' and *wen* 'fair' or 'blessed'. *Blodwen* is the title of a nineteenth-century Welsh opera by Joseph Parry. The love duet 'Hywel and Blodwen' remains popular to this day.

Bobi *m*
A Welsh spelling of Bobby from Robert. Bobi Jones is one of Wales' most distinguished men of letters.

Bodfan *m*
The saint of *Abergwyngregyn* in Gwynedd. Bodvan Anwyl was a pioneering Welsh lexicographer.

Bonner *
A surname from ab YNYR.

Bowen *
A surname from ab OWEN.

Brace *
A surname from the Welsh *bras* 'stout', 'fat'.

Bradwen *m*
One of ARTHUR's followers in the tale of *Culhwch ac Olwen*. Bradwen Jones was a composer of Welsh songs.

Braint *m*
The name of a noble and loyal servant from the early histories.

Brân *m*
A diminutive form of BENDIGEIDFRAN, a Celtic god and important character in the *Mabinogion* tales; also means 'crow'.

Brangwyn *
Possibly from the place name *Bryngwyn*. Sir Frank Brangwyn is the artist after whom the Brangwyn Hall in Swansea is named.

Branwen *f*
Sister of BRÂN and the tragic heroine of the second branch of the tales of the *Mabinogion*; praised for her beauty by the bards.

Breeze, Brice, Bryce *
Surnames derived from ap RHYS.

Brengain *f*
The name of a handmaiden in an early Welsh version of *Tristan and Isolde*.

Brenig, Brennig *m*
A river name and possible diminutive form of BRÂN.

Briallen *f*
The Welsh for 'primrose'.

Brianne *f*
From a Carmarthenshire place name (with the final 'e' pronounced).

Bron, Broni *f*
Diminutive forms of BRONWEN.

Bronwen *f*
A variant of BRANWEN; or from *bron* 'breast' and *wen* 'white', 'fair'. Bronwen Morgan is one of the main protagonists in the novel *How Green Was My Valley*.

Brwyn, Brwyno *m*
Names from early Welsh legend; also as in the place name *Cwm Brwyno*. Brwyn was the owner of a famous black horse in early Welsh tales.

Brychan *m*
An early prince who gave his name to *Brycheiniog* (Brecknockshire). Brychan Llŷr has been a lead singer with a number of Welsh pop groups.

Brymor *
A surname derived from BRYNMOR.

Bryn *m*
A diminutive form of BRYNMOR or Brinley. Bryn Terfel is the Welsh

baritone who has achieved world-wide fame as an opera star.

Brynach *m*
An early Celtic saint associated with a number of tales relating to place names on the borders of the present Carmarthenshire and Pembrokeshire.

Brynmor *m*
As in the place name *Bryn Mawr* 'large hill'. Brynmor Williams played scrum-half for Wales and the British Lions.

Brython *m*
The Welsh name for a Briton.

Buddug *f*
The Welsh form of the British Boudicca (Boadicea); also used as the Welsh for Victoria.

Bumffrey, Bumphrey *
Surnames derived from ap Humphrey .

Bunner *
A surname from ab YNYR.

Bunnion, Bunyan, Bunyon *
Surnames derived from ab EINION.

Byrnach *m*
A variant of BRYNACH.

C

Caddick, Caddock *
Surnames derived from CADOG.

Cadell *m*
The name of an early Celtic saint and a number of legendary heroes. Cadell was the name of the father of Hywel Dda, the lawmaker.

Cadfael *m*
The baptismal name of St Cadog. Brother Cadfael was the medieval monk detective hero of a series of books by Ellis Peters.

Cadfan *m*
A Celtic saint who established a monastery on Bardsey Island.

Cadi, Cati *f*
Diminutive forms of CATRIN. Cadi Haf was a character in traditional May Day celebrations.

Cadifor, Cydifor *m*
Variants of a name from the early genealogies and a ninth-century abbot of Llancarfan.

Cadnant *m*
The name of a number of rivers in north Wales.

Cadog *m*
The popular form of CADFAEL, a famous saint with many churches to his name.

Cadogan *
A surname based on CADWGAN.

Cadwalader *
A surname and first name variant
of CADWALADR.

Cadwaladr m
An early name made up of *cad*
'battle' and *gwaladr* 'leader'.
Famed as a protector of his people, Cadwaladr is also ascribed
with saintly qualities. Betsi
Cadwaladr was dubbed the Welsh
Florence Nightingale for her work
in nursing wounded soldiers.

Cadwallon m
A king of Gwynedd who fought
Edwin of Northumbria in the seventh century. One of his sons was
named CADFAEL and another
CADWALADR. His court poet was
named Afan Ferddig.

Cadwgan m
A name from the early history of
south Wales and the Welsh Bishop
of Bangor who was consecrated
during the reign of Llywelyn
(Fawr) in the thirteenth century.

Cadwy m
The legendary son of GERAINT in
the Arthurian legend.

Caeo m
A parish name from Car-
marthenshire. Julian Cayo Evans
was a leader of the Free Wales
Army during the 1960s.

Caerwyn m
A variant of CARWYN. Caerwyn
Williams was a highly respected
academic and man of letters.

Cai m
One of the Welsh ARTHUR's two faithful and heroic companions. He was
endowed with a number of magical
attributes which suggest a derivation
from a Celtic god. He lost many of
his heroic and magical qualities by
the time he became the peevish Kay
of the English romances.

Caian m
A son of BRYCHAN and early Celtic
saint.

Caio m
A variant of CAEO.

Caledfryn m
The bardic name of one William
Willams, a poet and eisteddfod ad-
judicator in the latter part of the
nineteenth century.

Callwen f
A saintly daughter of BRYCHAN
whose name is commemorated in
the Ceredigion village of *Cellan*.

Cam, Gam, Games *
Surnames from the Welsh *cam*
which when used after personal
names originally referred to the
owner's 'squint'.

Camwy m
A river in Patagonia.

Caradog *m*
The Welsh form of the British leader, Caratacus, famed for his valour and resistance to the Romans. Although defeated, captured and taken to Rome, his noble presence gained for him an Emperor's pardon. Caradog was the bardic name of Griffith Rhys Jones, conductor of the massed choirs of protesting south Wales miners.

Caredig *m*
A variant of CEREDIG.

Cari *f*
An affectionate diminutive form of CERIDWEN.

Carn, Carne *
Surnames from a place name incorporating *carn*, the Welsh for 'cairn'.

Caron *m*
The saint's name as found in *Tregaron* in Ceredigion.

Caronwen *f*
A combination of the saint's name and *wen* meaning 'fair', 'pure' or 'blessed'.

Carrog *m and f*
A fairly common river name or place name meaning 'torrent'.

Carwen *f*
A girl's name made up of *câr* 'love' and *wen* 'blessed'.

Carwyn *m*
The masculine version of CARWEN. Carwyn James was an inspirational rugby coach for Llanelli and the British Lions.

Caryl *f*
From the Welsh *câr* meaning 'love'. Caryl Parry Jones is a popular and versatile singer and entertainer.

Carys *f*
From the Welsh *câr* meaning 'love'.

Casnar *m*
A warrior from early Welsh tradition, proverbial for his delight in war.

Cati *f*
A diminutive form of CATRIN. Twm Siôn Cati was a historical figure who was turned into 'the wild wag of Wales'. He was the hero of a trilogy of novels by the Welsh author T Llew Jones.

Catrin *f*
The Welsh form of Catherine. Catrin of Berain was related to Harri Tudor and famous for four marriages, the progeny of which made her an ancestor to many of the noble families of north Wales.

Cecil *
It is a surprise to learn that what would seem to be the most English of names was originally a sur-

name from the Welsh name SEISYLL.

Cedwyn *m*
An early saint commemorated in a number of place names. In legend, one of the seven who escaped from ARTHUR's last battle at Camlan.

Cefni *m*
A river name as found in *Llangefni* in Anglesey; used as a bardic name.

Ceian *m*
A fictitious hero created by Iolo Morganwg (*see* IOLO).

Ceidiog *m*
A form of Ceidio, an early Celtic saint and river name in Gwynedd. It is also the name of one of the men of the old North that the poet Aneirin commemorated in the sixth century.

Ceidrych *m*
A river in Carmarthenshire and a name adopted by the writer Keidrych Rees.

Ceindeg *f*
From *cain* 'fair' and *teg* 'beautiful'. She is listed in Welsh tradition as a daughter of Llywarch Hen, who gained fame through his sons.

Ceinwen *f*
The saint of *Llangeinwen*; from Cain, a daughter of BRYCHAN and *wen* 'holy'. A tale is told of her settling in a place of serpents which

were miraculously turned into stones, these being the ammonite fossils by Keynsham in Somerset.

Ceiriog *m*
The name of a river in the former Clwyd adopted as a bardic name by one of the most popular poets of the nineteenth century, John Ceiriog Hughes.

Ceirios *f*
The Welsh for 'cherry'.

Ceiro *m*
A stream and place name from Ceredigion.

Ceitho *m*
The saint of *Llangeitho* in Ceredigion and one of the five saints of *Pumsaint*, a place name meaning 'five saints', and *Llanpumsaint*, a place name meaning 'church of the five saints'. The saints are GWYN, GWYNNO, GWYNORO, Ceitho and CELYNIN.

Cellan *m*
The name of a village in Ceredigion. James Cellan-Jones was a notable broadcaster. *See also* CALLWEN.

Celyn *m*
The Welsh for 'holly'; also the name of a drowned village commemorated in the lake name *Llyn Celyn*.

Celynin, Celynen *m*
Variants of the name of another of the five saints of *Pumsaint* and

Llanpumsaint (Gwyn, Gwynno, Gwynoro, Ceitho and Celynin).

Cemais *m*
From the Anglesey place name; originally from *cam* 'crooked', recording the meandering bends of a river.

Cennard *m*
Possibly a variant of the place name *Cenarth* in Carmarthenshire. Cennard Davies has done much to develop and promote the teaching of Welsh as a second language.

Cennydd *m*
The name of an early Celtic saint to be found in the place name *Senghennydd*.

Cenwyn *m*
A boy's name containing *wyn* 'blessed'.

Ceredig *m*
The ruler who gave his name to the present county of Ceredigion.

Ceri *f and m*
An old name originally from *Câr* and *i* (Car's land); also a river name. Ceri Richards was an important abstract painter who received international recognition.

Cerian *f and m*
A variant of Ceri.

Ceridwen *f*
A powerful sorceress, and an im-portant figure in the Taliesin legend. She was also the mother of Afagddu, the ugliest man in the world.

Ceris, Cerys *f and m*
A personal name found in old legal documents. *Pwll Ceris* (Ceris Pool) is the name of a whirlpool in the Menai Straits. Cerys Matthews is lead singer with the pop group Catatonia.

Cerith *m*
A variant of Ceri.

Cethin *
A surname from the adjective *cethin* meaning 'swarthy' or 'roan' when applied to horses.

Cian *m*
The name of a Welsh poet from the sixth century, also acclaimed as *Gwenith Gwawd* (Wheat of Song), and the name of an early saint. Cian Clowes is a member of the pop group Super Furry Animals.

Cilmin *m*
Known as Droed-ddu (Blackfoot), Cilmin is said to have stolen a book of spells from a demon. In the process of flight, he plunged his leg into a stream upon which it turned black.

Cilydd *m*
A legendary name and father of the beautiful Olwen, the quest for

whose hand is told in the tale of *Culhwch ac Olwen*.

Cled *m*
A diminutive form of CLEDWYN.

Cledan *m*
From river names in Powys and Ceredigion.

Cledlyn *m*
A bardic name and stream in Ceredigion.

Cledwyn *m*
A river name from the former Denbighshire. Lord Cledwyn of Penrhos was Labour Secretary of State for Wales.

Clough *
A surname from the adjective *cloff* meaning 'lame'. Sir Clough Williams-Ellis was an architect whose most famous creation is probably the 'Italian' village of Portmeirion.

Clwyd *f and m*
As in *Dyffryn Clwyd* (The Vale of Clwyd) in north Wales. Hafina Clwyd is a contemporary journalist and broadcaster.

Clynnog *m*
A village in Gwynedd from *celyn* meaning 'holly'.

Cogan *
A surname based on a place name between Cardiff and Penarth and itself most probably a contraction of CADWGAN.

Collen *m*
The saint of *Llangollen* and the Welsh for 'hazel'. Collen is also associated with churches in Cornwall and Ireland.

Colwyn *m*
As in the place name in former county ofClwyd.

Conway *
A surname from the town on the River Conwy.

Cothi *f and m*
A river name from Carmarthenshire; Siân Cothi is a well-known singer of both popular and classical music.

Cradoc, Craddock *
Surnames derived from CARADOG.

Cranogwen *f*
A feminine bardic name linked to *Llangrannog*. Cranogwen was a formidable early feminist.

Creiddylad *f*
'The maiden of most majesty that was ever in the Island of Britain'. Her name equates to Cordelia, the youngest daughter of Llŷr, i.e. Shakespeare's 'Lear', King of Britain.

Creirwy *f*
Daughter of CERIDWEN and, accord-

ing to legend, the fairest maiden in the world.

Creunant *m*
A Glamorgan village name. Alun Creunant Davies was the first director of the Welsh Books Council.

Crwys *m*
A bardic name from the Welsh for a 'cross'. William Crwys Williams was a popular lyric poet and Eisteddfodic Archdruid.

Cule *
A surname from the adjective *cul* meaning 'narrow' or 'thin'.

Culhwch *m*
The hero who invoked the help of King ARTHUR to accomplish the tasks necessary to win the hand of OLWEN in the tale of *Culhwch ac Olwen*.

Curig *m*
The name of an early warrior turned Celtic saint as commemorated in *Llangurig*.

Custennin, Cystennin *m*
The Welsh for Constantine. *See also* CYSTENNIN.

Cwyfan *m*
An early Celtic saint associated with Anglesey.

Cybi *m*
A Celtic saint whose name is found

in the place name *Caergybi* (Holyhead). Tradition has it that Cybi faced east in the morning and west in the evening and so had a tanned face and was known as Cybi Felyn (Yellow Cybi). *See also* SEIRIOL.

Cyfeiliog *m*
An old administrative district in Montgomeryshire. It derives from a personal name such as CYNFAEL and meant 'Cy(n)fael's land'. Iorwerth Cyfeiliog Peate was the founder and first curator of the Welsh Folk Museum at St Fagans.

Cyffin, Kyffin *m* *
A forename and surname from the Welsh *cyffin* meaning 'boundary' or 'border'. Kyffin Williams is a highly respected artist who has captured on canvas the people and places of his native north Wales.

Cynan *m*
A popular name from among the old rulers of Wales. It was also the poetic name of Albert Evans-Jones, a poet and archdruid who transformed the National Eisteddfod of Wales.

Cyndeyrn *m*
A sixth-century Celtic saint; the St Kentigern of Scotland.

Cynddylan *m*
A seventh-century lord of

Pengwern in Powys, whose death is lamented in verse by his sister HELEDD. 'Cynddylan on a Tractor' is one of a series of poems by R S Thomas.

Cynddylig *m*
One of the sons of LLYWARCH Hen whose death is lamented in early Welsh poems; also the title of a poem by the twentieth-century poet T Gwynn Jones.

Cynfab *m*
An early saint commemorated at *Capel Cynfab* in Carmarthenshire.

Cynfael, Cynfal *m*
Variants of a river name from Gwynedd, and one of the three British kings slain at the Battle of Dyrham in Gloucester in 577. *See also* CYFEILIOG.

Cynfelin, Cynfelyn *m*
Variants of an early Celtic saint whose name is found in the place name *Llangynfelyn* in Ceredigion; also an early hero who lost his life at the Battle of Catraeth c. 580.

Cynfrig, Cynrig *m*
Variants of a popular name in early Welsh genealogies; and also a Breckon river name.

Cynfyn *m*
The name of an early king of *Erging* or Archenfield between the Rivers Monnow and Wye which today lies within the boundaries of the former county of Hereford.

Cynin *m*
An early Celtic saint as in the place name *Llangynin*.

Cynlais *m*
The name of the river as found in *Ystradgynlais*.

Cynog *m*
An early Celtic saint associated with Brecknockshire. Cynog Dafis is a former Plaid Cymru MP for Ceredigion and current Assembly Member.

Cynon *m*
A Glamorgan river name, and an early British hero. There was also an early Celtic saint of this name.

Cynwal *m*
A heroic name from the earliest Welsh poetry.

Cynwyl *m*
An early Celtic saint associated with Brecknockshire; also a place name in Carmarthenshire.

Cynyr *m*
The name of St David's grandfather.

Cystennin *m*
A variant of CUSTENNIN. Constantinople is known as *Caer Gystennin* in Welsh.

D

Dafi *m*
An older diminutive form of
DAFYDD.

Dafina *f*
A Welsh spelling of the Scottish
name Davina or, like Davina, a
feminine form of DAFI.

Dafydd *m*
The Welsh form of the Biblical
David. Dafydd ap Gwilym was the
greatest Welsh poet of his era.
Dafydd y Garreg Wen was a legendary harpist and is the name of
a popular Welsh song.

Dai *m*
The south Wales affectionate di-
minutive form of David. Dai
Dower was a famous boxer, Dai
Rees a golfer and a Dai cap is that
characteristically Welsh flat cap.

Dalis *m*
There was a famous horse fair
called *Ffair Dalis* which was held
at Lampeter. Recently the fair has
been resurrected but more as a car-
nival day than a horse fair.

Dathan *m*
A male variant of TATHAN.

Davy, Davies *
Surnames derived from DAFYDD,
one of the Welsh forms of David,
DEWI being the other.

Day, Daye *
Surnames formed from DAI or DEI,
both colloquial abbreviations of
DAFYDD.

Dedwydd *f and m*
The Welsh for 'content'.

Dee *
A surname from the adjective *du*
meaning 'black' (referring originally to the colour of the hair).
Thus the famous Dr John Dee was
the original 'Black Jack'.

Deganwy *m*
As in the town on the north Wales
coast.

Degwel *m*
A form of the name Dogfael or
Dogmael, the saint who gave his
name to *St Dogmaels* near Cardigan.

Dei *m*
The north Wales affectionate diminutive form of David. Dei Thomas is a popular broadcaster and
presenter.

Deian *m*
An affectionate diminutive form of

DAFYDD. *Deian a Loli* is the title of a popular novel by Kate Roberts.

Deiniol *m*
An early Celtic saint of noble lineage, associated with Bangor; the Welsh Daniel.

Delfryn *m*
From *del* 'pretty' and *bryn* 'hill'.

Delwen *f*
A feminine form of DELWYN.

Delwyn *m*
From *del* 'pretty' and *gwyn* 'fair'. Delwyn Siôn is a contemporary pop singer and producer.

Delyth *f*
From *del* 'pretty'. Marian Delyth is a professional photographer.

Derec *m*
A variant of Derek. Derec Llwyd Morgan is a distinguished academic and man of letters.

Derfel *m*
An early Celtic saint who was also one of the survivors of Arthur's last battle at Camlan. A famous wooden statue of Derfel at *Llandderfel* in Merioneth, was destroyed in 1538 on the orders of Thomas Cromwell.

Deri *m*
A plural form of *derw* meaning 'oak'.

Derwen *m*
The Welsh for 'oak tree'.

Derwenna *f*
A feminine form of DERWEN.

Derwydd *m*
The Welsh for 'druid'.

Derwyn *m*
A variant of DERWEN. Derwyn Jones played in the second row for Cardiff and Wales.

Deryn *f*
The Welsh for 'bird'.

Deudraeth *m*
A bardic name from the place name *Penrhyndeudraeth*. Gwilym Deudraeth was the poetic name of one William Edwards.

Deulwyn *m*
From *llwyn* meaning 'grove'.

Devonald *
A surname from the Welsh name DYFNWAL.

Dewey *
A surname, possibly from the place name *Llanddewi*, which refers to DEWI (David) the patron saint of Wales.

Dewi *m*
One of the Welsh names for David, the patron saint of Wales, whose feast day falls on the first day in March. Dewi Prys Thomas was an influential architect. Dewi Pws is an entertainer, singer and comedian.

Dilwen *f*
A recombination of *Dil* from DILYS and *wen* meaning 'fair'.

Dilwyn *m*
The masculine form of DILWEN. John Dilwyn Llewelyn was a pioneering Welsh photographer of the early nineteenth century.

Dilys *f*
The Welsh for 'genuine'. Dilys Cadwaladr was the first woman to win the crown at the National Eisteddfod in 1953. Dilys Powell was a well-known film critic.

Dinmael *m*
A place name associated with Merioneth, from *din* meaning 'fort' and *mael* meaning 'prince'.

Doiran *m*
Although it sounds Welsh, Doiran is not a Welsh name but rather an area in Selonica. Two Welsh soldiers serving there under fire undertook to name their first child after the area were they to survive the horrors of the First World War.

Dona *f*
A form of Dôn, a Celtic goddess associated with the River Danube. The sons of Dôn play a prominent part in the tales of the *Mabinogion*.

Dulais *m*
A river name as found in the place name *Pontarddulais*. Dulais Rhys is the name of a contemporary Welsh composer.

Dwyfan *m*
A masculine form of DWYFOR.

Dwyfor *f*
A river name in Gwynedd, taken as part of his title by the Earl Lloyd George.

Dwynwen *f*
A daughter of BRYCHAN, the patron saint of lovers whose feast day, January 25th, is the Welsh equivalent of St Valentine's Day.

Dwyryd *f and m*
A river name in Gwynedd.

Dwysan *f*
A combination of *dwys* meaning 'serious' and *an*, an affectionate diminutive.

Dwysli *f*
The Welsh equivalent of Dulcie.

Dyddgu *f*
The dark-haired, unattainable beauty of the poems of Dafydd ap Gwilym. Dyddgu Owen was the author of a number of novels for children.

Dyfan *m*
An early Welsh saint and a river name. Dyfan Roberts is a well-known actor.

Dyfed *m*
An ancient kingdom in southwest Wales.

Dyfi *f and m*
The name of a Gwynedd river which flows to the sea at *Aberdyfi*.

Dyfnallt *m*
A bardic name. Dyfnallt Morgan was a writer and broadcaster.

Dyfnwal *m*
A fifth-century ruler of Britain said to have codified its laws and measured the length and breadth of the Island.

Dyfri *m*
From *dyfri*, a combination of *dwfr* 'water' and *thi* 'lord', as in the place name *Llanymddyfri* (Llandovery).

Dyfrig *m*
A fifth-century Celtic saint and important religious leader in southeast Wales.

Dyfyr *f*
With ENID and TEGAU, Dyfyr was one of the 'Three Splendid Maidens' of King ARTHUR's Court who was often referred to by the poets as a standard of beauty.

Dylan *m*
A mythical character from the tales of the *Mabinogion*, and one of Wales' most famous latter-day poets, Dylan Thomas.

E

Ebrill *f*
The Welsh for 'April'.

Edern *m*
A name from the earliest genealogies, Edeirnion, meaning 'Edern's land'. Edern ap NUDD is a knight who appears in a number of the Arthurian romances.

Edmwnd *m*
The Welsh form of Edmund. Edmwnd Prys was an important figure in the Welsh Renaissance of the sixteenth century.

Ednyfed *m*
A name from the early Welsh genealogies, as found in

Trefednyfed in Anglesey. Ednyfed Hudson Davies was a one-time Labour MP.

Edryd *m*
A name from the early annals of Welsh history.

Edwards *
Edward was one of the regal names adopted when the old patronymic system was falling into disuse. To this was added the genitive 's of the English system of surnames.

Efa *f*
The Welsh form of the Biblical Eve, wife of Adam.

Efanna *f*
A variant of IFANNA.

Efnysien *m*
The half-brother of BRÂN and the villain of the second branch of the tales of the *Mabinogion* who caused enmity between Wales and Ireland.

Efrog *m*
The name of a fictitious king of Britain in the first century BC, a man of great stature and wonderful strength. Efrog is the Welsh name for York.

Egham *
A surname from the Welsh *fychan* meaning 'the younger' which also gave the surname Vaughan.

Egryn *m*
The saint's name found in *Llanegryn,* Merioneth; also the ancestor of a line of princes in Powys.

Eic *m*
A diminutive form of the Biblical Eisac or Isaac.

Eiddwen *f*
A lake in Ceredigion. Eiddwen Harry is an opera singer.

Eifion *m*
The name found in *Eifionydd,* a region of Gwynedd.

Eifiona *f*
A feminine form of EIFION.

Eigr *f*
The mother of the Welsh ARTHUR and the greatest beauty of her time.

Eigra *f*
A form of EIGR. Eigra Lewis Roberts is an important contemporary novelist and writer of short stories.

Eilian *f and m*
The saint commemorated in *Llaneilian,* Anglesey

Eilir, Eilyr *f and m*
A name created by Iolo Morganwg (*see* IOLO).

Eiluned *f*
A variant of ELUNED.

Eilwen *f*
From *ail* 'just like' and *wen* 'fair' or 'beautiful'.

Eilwyn *m*
A masculine form of EILWEN, or maybe a variant of AELWYN.

Einion *m*
The Welsh for 'anvil' as in the place name *Caereinion,* and a name from early history. Einion Evans won the chair in the National Eisteddfod of 1983 with a poignant poem in memory of his daughter ENNIS.

Einon, Ennion, Eynon *
Surnames derived from EINION.

Eira *f*
The Welsh for 'snow'.

Eirian *f and m*
A Welsh word meaning 'splendid', 'bright' or 'fair'. J Eirian Davies was a poet and Jennie Eirian, his wife, was an influential editor and newspaper writer. The author, Siôn Eirian, is their son.

Eiriana *f*
A feminine variant of EIRIAN.

Eirianedd *f*
A Welsh word meaning 'brightness', 'splendour' or 'beauty'. A feminine variant of EIRIAN.

Eirianwen *f*
A combination of EIRIAN with the ending *wen*.

Eirig *m*
A variant of EIRUG.

Eiriol *f*
A Welsh word meaning 'snowy' or 'snow-white'.

Eirlys *f*
The Welsh for 'snowdrop'.

Eirug *m*
From the Welsh for 'bold'. Eirug Wyn is a contemporary, innovative Welsh writer.

Eirwen *f*
'Snow-white' from *eira* 'snow' and *wen* 'white'. Eirwen Gwynn is a literary figure who wrote about scientific matters.

Eirwyn *m*
A masculine form of EIRWEN. Eirwyn Pontshân was a unique Cardiganshire teller of surreal and hilarious tales.

Eiry *f*
From eira meaning 'snow' or a diminutive form of EIRIANWEN. Eiry Palfrey is an author who has specialised in books for Welsh learners.

Eiryl *m*
A variant of EURYL.

Elain *f*
A word meaning 'a fawn'.

Elan *f*
One of the three daughters of the Celtic goddess Dôn and a river name. Elan Closs Stephens currently chairs S4C (the Welsh language Channel Four television station).

Eldryd, Eldrydd *f and m*
Welsh versions of a Saxon name.

Elen, Elin, Elena *f*
The Welsh Helen of Troy, a name which appears in the earliest annals.

Elenid, Elenydd *f*
The highland area in which the Rivers Wye, Severn, TYWI, TEIFI and Ystwyth have their source.

Eleri *f*
A king's daughter and river name in Ceredigion.

Elerydd *m*
A masculine form of ELERI and the bardic name of the poet and former Archdruid, W J Gruffydd.

Elfed *m*
The name of an ancient kingdom in the area around present-day Leeds; and also a bardic name. Elfed Lewis was an inspirational balladeer and folk singer.

Elfryn *m*
A word derived from *bryn* 'hill'.

Elfyn *m*
A bardic name. Elfyn Pritchard is an author and educationalist.

Elgan *m*
A heroic name that appears in the early genealogies. Elgan Philip Davies is the author of a number of 'whodunits' and popular novels for children.

Elgar *m*
An early name as found in *Drefelgarn* in Pembrokeshire.

Elian *m*
An early Celtic saint.

Elias, Elis, Ellis *
As surnames, it is suggested that these are more likely to have come from an early Welsh name, ELISE, rather than the Biblical names Elias (Elijah) and Eliseus (Elisha).

Elidan *f*
The saint in the place name *Llanelidan* in the Vale of Llangollen; perhaps a variant of St ILID, mother of CURIG.

Elidir *m*
A fictitious saint and king of Britain.

Elin *f*
A variant of ELEN. Elin ap Hywel is a contemporary poet, writer and editor with a women's publishing house.

Elinor *f*
The Welsh form of Eleanor. Elinor Bennett is a highly respected harpist.

Elise *m*
A frequent name in the early annals, the most famous being a king of seventh-century Powys who had a pillar erected in his honour in the Vale of Llangollen.

Elliw *f*
The original name was Ellylw but it has come down through the genealogies as Elliw. Elliw was one of the ladies of ARTHUR's court in the tale of *Culhwch ac Olwen*.

Elonwy *f*
A variant of AELONWY.

Eluned, Luned *f*
Welsh forms of Lynette. Eluned Morgan was a literary figure who

was born in 1870 aboard ship on a
voyage to Patagonia.

Elvis *m*
The saint of *Llaneilfyw* (St Elvis)
called Eilfyw in Welsh, a fifth-century Celtic saint who might well
have been a cousin to St David according to the genealogies.

Elwyn *m*
A variant of ALWYN, but there was
also a Cornish saint of this name.
John Elwyn was an innovative and
important Welsh painter.

Elystan *m*
The Welsh form of Aethelstan. The
ninth-century Elystan Glodrydd
(the Renowned) was head of one
of the Five Royal Tribes of Wales.
Lord Elystan Morgan is a Labour
peer.

Elysteg *f*
A feminine form of Eliseg (an ancient king of Powys).

Emlyn *m*
An early Dyfed place name from
am 'surrounding' and *glyn* 'the valley'. Emlyn Williams was a famous actor and playwright.

Emrys *m*
The Welsh form of Ambrose.
Emrys Bowen was a notable geog-
rapher.

Emyr *m*
The Welsh for 'emperor' or

'king'. Emyr Humphreys is a
distinguished man of letters who
writes in both English and
Welsh.

Endaf *m*
Endaf Emlyn is the name of a
popular singer and television producer.

Enfys *f*
The Welsh for 'rainbow'.

Enid *f*
The wife of GERAINT in Arthurian
romance, praised for her beauty by
the bards. Enid Blyton was a popular author of children's adventure
tales.

Ennis *f*
Ennis Evans was a promising literary talent who died at an early
age.

Eos *m*
The Welsh for a 'nightingale' and
soubriquet for a singer.

Erfyl *f and m*
Originally the saint commemorated in the place name *Llanerfyl*
in Powys. Gwyn Erfyl is a highly
respected broadcaster.

Erin *f*
An old name for Ireland.

Erwyd *m*
As found in the place name
Ponterwyd in Ceredigion. Erwyd

Howells is a Ceredigion shepherd and a contemporary collector of folklore who writes and broadcasts on local radio.

Eryl *f and m*
The Welsh word for a 'hunt' or 'chase'.

Eryn *f*
A variant of ERIN.

Esyllt *f*
The Welsh Isolde, lover of TRYSTAN and a bardic standard of beauty.

Ethall, Ethell *
Surnames derived from ITHEL.

Ethni *f*
A name adopted from Irish legend, the mother of MELANGELL.

Eudaf *m*
A legendary prince of north Wales.

Eunydd *m*
A name from the tales of the *Mabinogion*. Eunydd appears as one of the children of the goddess Dôn.

Eurddyl *f*
A sister of URIEN, an ancient ruler of the Britons.

Eurfron *f*
TEGAU Eurfron (golden breast) was considered to be the model of wifely fidelity by the bards.

Eurfryn *m*
A male variant of the name EURFRON.

Eurfyl *m*
A variant of ERFYL.

Eurfyl *f*
A variant of GWERFYL.

Eurgain *f*
The legendary sister of Joseph of Arimathea; also the saint of *Llaneurgain.*

Eurig *m*
A variant of EIRUG.

Eurof *m*
From *aur* 'gold' and *gof* 'smith'.

Euron *f*
A legendary beauty and enchant-ress.

Euronwy *f*
With CERIDWEN and EURON, Euronwy was one of 'the three legendary enchantresses of the Isle of Britain'.

Euros *m*
A diminutive of EUROSWYDD.

Euroswydd *m*
The father of EFNYSIEN in the tales of the *Mabinogion.*

Eurwen *f*
From *aur* 'gold' and *wen* 'white', 'fine'.

Eurwyn *m*
A masculine variant of EURWEN.

Euryl *m*
A variant of EURYN. *See also*
EIRYL.

Euryn *m*
From *aur* 'gold' and also *eurin*
'golden' or 'magnificent'.

Eurys *m*
From *aur* 'gold' as EURYN. Eurys
Rowlands was a Welsh academic.

Evans *
A surname derived from IEUAN or
IFAN.

Eynon *
A surname derived from EINON.

F

Faleiry *f*
The Welsh form of Valerie.

Fanw *f*
A diminutive form of MYFANWY.

Ffion *f*
The Welsh for 'foxgloves'. Ffion is
the name of the wife of the Con-
servative Party leader, William
Hague.

Fflamddwyn *m*
The Welsh for a 'flame-bearer'
and the name given to one of the
tribal chiefs against whom OWAIN
and URIEN fought in the sixth century.

Fflur *f*
One of the three loved ones famed
for their beauty by the bards. Also
found in the place name *Ystrad
Fflur* (anglicised as Strata Florida)
meaning 'wide valley' or 'plain of
flowers'.

Ffolant, Folant *f and m*
The Welsh name for Valentine, as
in St Valentine's Day.

Ffowc *m*
The Welsh form of Foulke. Islwyn
Ffowc Elis is the author of the book
chosen as the Welsh book of the
century, *Cysgod y Cryman.*

Ffraid *f*
Welsh form of St Brigit or St Bride,
the saint of *Llansanffraid* in
Ceredigion.

Ffrancon *m*
As found in the place name *Nant
Ffrancon*, possibly from *ffranc,* an
early word for 'mercenary soldier'.

Fioled *f*
The Welsh form of the name Violet.

Floyd *m* *
A variant of Lloyd from the original LLWYD.

Fychan *m*
The adjective meaning 'small' or, in the case of personal names, 'the younger' which has been anglicised to Vaughan.

G

Gaenor, Gaynor *f*
A name derived from GWENHWYFAR, King ARTHUR's beautiful wife, Guinevere.

Galâth *m*
The Welsh Galahad, son of Lancelot, and the epitome of the knight in shining armour in search of the Holy Grail.

Gam, Games *
Surnames derived from *cam* 'crooked'.

Garan *m*
A Welsh river name found in the place name *Llangaran* (Llangarren), from the Welsh for 'heron'.

Gareth *m*
One of the knights of ARTHUR's round table and brother of GWALCHMAI. Gareth Edwards is one of the finest scrum halves to have played the game of rugby football.

Garin *m*
A variant of GARAN. Garin Jenkins plays rugby for Swansea and Wales.

Garmon *m*
An early saint associated with Powys, and sometimes associated with St Germanus who was sent to Britain in the late fourth century to combat heresy.

Garnon *m*
A Pembrokeshire name probably originally derived from the Old French for 'moustache'.

Garth *m*
The Welsh for 'promontory' or 'head'.

Garwen *f*
From *gar* 'leg' and *wen* 'fair', a name that appears in early commemorative stanzas and the triads where Garwen is listed as one of the mistresses of King ARTHUR.

Garwy *m*
Garwy was known to the poets as a valiant lover of singular renown.

Garwyn *m*
A king of Powys in the sixth century.

Gaynor *f*
A variant of GAENOR.

Generys *f*
A name from the bardic tradition,

one of the lovers of the poet-prince, Hywel ab Owain Gwynedd.

Geraint *m*
The hero of one of the Arthurian romances and also the name of the last independent king of Dumnonia (Devon) in the eighth century. Geraint Evans was an operatic baritone of international renown.

Gerallt *m*
Welsh for the name Gerald. Gerallt Gymro (Giraldus Cambrensis) travelled through Wales in the twelfth century and wrote an interesting portrait of the times and his fellow Welshmen.

Gerwyn *m*
A variant of GARWYN.

Gethin *m*
Perhaps from *cethin* meaning 'swarthy'. Rhys Gethin was a lieutenant of Owain GLYNDŴR.

Gildas *m*
An early saint linked with what is now Scotland, and the author of one of the earliest histories of Britain, written c. 559.

Gilfaethwy *m*
The son of Dôn who appears in the tales of the *Mabinogion*. He is infatuated with GOEWIN, and calls on his magician brother GWYDION to help arrange his violation of her. All the complications surrounding

this are the subject of the tale of *Math fab Mathonwy*.

Gittins, Gittings *
A surname derived from GUTO.

Gladys *f*
A variant of GWLADYS.

Glain *f*
The Welsh for a 'jewel'.

Glandeg *f and m*
The Welsh for 'beautiful' or 'fair'.

Glanffrwd *m*
A bardic name linked with *Llanwynno* in Glamorgan.

Glanmor *m*
A bardic name. Sir Glanmor Williams is a highly acclaimed historian.

Glannant *m*
Probably derived from a farm or place name.

Glascurion *m*
A legendary harpist referred to by Chaucer.

Glasnant *m*
Probably from a farm or place name containing *glas* 'blue' and *nant* 'stream'.

Glenda *f*
From *glân* 'fair' or 'holy' and *da* 'good'. Glenda Jackson is an actress turned politician.

Glenys f
From *glân* meaning 'fair' or 'holy'.
Glenys Kinnock is a Labour Member of the European Parliament.

Glesni f
From *glas* meaning 'blue'.

Gloyw m
As in *Caerloyw*, the Welsh for Gloucester. 'Gloyw of the Abundant Hair' is a character in the early histories and appears in the tales of the *Mabinogion*.

Glwyddyn m
Glwyddyn the craftsman was the builder of King ARTHUR's Hall.

Glyn m
The Welsh for 'vale' or 'valley' and a diminutive form of GLYNDWR. Glyn Daniel was a prominent archaeologist and Glyn Houston a popular actor.

Glyndŵr m
Owain Glyndŵr was a fifteenth-century Welsh prince and national hero, celebrated to this day. (It is pronounced with the accent on *dŵr*.)

Glyndwr m
A variant of GLYNDŴR but without the 'ŵ' and with the accent on *Glyn*.

Glynis f
A variant of GLENYS. Glynis Johns was a famous film star.

Glynog m
A variant of CLYNNOG. Glynog Dafis is a contemporary journalist and broadcaster.

Goewyn, Goewin f
Variants of the name of a maidservant in the tales of the *Mabinogion*.

Gofan m
An early Celtic saint commemorated at *St Gowan* in Pembrokeshire.

Goleu f
A daughter of BRYCHAN.

Goleuddydd f
The mother of CULHWCH and wife of CILYDD in the tale of *Culhwch ac Olwen*.

Golwg Hafddydd f
Meaning 'the appearance of a summer's day', Golwg Hafddydd is the name of a handmaiden in the tale of *Trystan ac Esyllt*.

Gomer m
A grandson of the Biblical Noah, adopted as a bardic name. Gwasg Gomer (The Gomerian Press) is a leading Welsh publishing house.

Gooch *
A surname from *coch* meaning 'red'.

Goronw m
A variant of GRONWY.

Goronwy *m*
The most popular form of the original GRONWY. Goronwy Owen was an eighteenth-century tragic and heroic bardic figure associated with Anglesey.

Gorwel *m*
The Welsh for 'horizon'.

Gough *
A surname from *coch* meaning 'red'.

Griff *m*
A diminutive form of GRUFFUDD. Griff Rhys Jones is a popular comedian and television personality.

Griffin, Griffiths *
Surnames derived from GRUFFUDD.

Griffith *m*
A variant of GRUFFUDD. Griffith Jones was the religious reformer who established a system of circulating schools during the eighteenth century.

Griffri *m*
The name of a prince, found in the genealogies of the kings of *Brycheiniog* (Brecknockshire).

Gronwy, Gronw *m*
Gronw Pefr fell in love with BLODEUWEDD and plotted to kill her husband in the third branch of the tales from the *Mabinogion*.

Gruff *m*
A diminutive form of GRUFFUDD.

Gruff Rhys is lead singer with the pop group Super Furry Animals.

Gruffudd *m*
The name of a number of Welsh kings and princes. Gruffudd ap LLYWELYN, who died in 1063, was the one native Welsh king to rule the whole of Wales.

Gruffydd *m*
A variant of GRUFFUDD. William John Gruffydd is a name shared by two twentieth-century Welsh poets, one of whom was a professor of Welsh at the University of Cardiff, the other a minister of religion and Eisteddfodic Archdruid.

Grug *f*
The Welsh for 'heather'.

Gurwyn *m*
A masculine variant of the form found in the place name *Gwauncaegurwen*.

Guto *m*
An affectionate diminutive form of GRUFFUDD. Guto Nyth Brân was a legendary runner associated with the parish of Llanwonno. He once had trouble rounding up a little grey sheep, which turned out to be a hare.

Gutyn, Gutun *m*
Affectionate diminutives of GRUFFUDD.

Gwair, Gweir m
A knight of sad disposition in the Arthurian legend.

Gwalchmai m
Gawain in the French romances. Gwalchmai was one of the most famous of King ARTHUR's heroic knights. He was the best of walkers and of riders, he never returned without having completed his quest, and he was one of the three most courteous men to guests and strangers.

Gwalia f
The Latin for Wales. *Gwalia Wen* (Fair Gwalia) is a poetic term for Wales.

Gwarnant m
A variant of *garwnant/garnant* meaning 'turbulent stream', which is found in place names.

Gwawl m
The man in the first tale of the *Mabinogion* who tricked the hero PWYLL into giving him his proposed wife Rhiannon, and who in turn was tricked by RHIANNON and Pwyll into giving her back to Pwyll.

Gwawr f
Both CEREDIG and BRYCHAN had daughters of this name. The name means 'dawn' in English.

Gweirfyl f
A variant of GWERFYL.

Gweirydd m
With GARETH, a brother of GWALCHMAI in the Arthurian romances. Gweirydd ap Rhys was the bardic name of a nineteenth-century Welsh writer.

Gwen f
The name means 'fair' or 'blessed' in English. It could be a diminutive form of GWEN-HWYFAR or GWENLLIAN. It is a name that appears frequently in the early annals. *Gwen Tomos* is the title of a popular novel by Daniel Owen.

Gwên m
The last and favourite of LLYWARCH Hen's twenty-four sons, all of whom were killed in battle.

Gwenallt m
A bardic name derived from the place name *Alltwen*. Gwenallt Jones was the poet who wrote with passion of the lot of the working man in the industrial south of Wales in the early twentieth century.

Gwenant f
The feminine form of GWYNANT comprising of *gwen* 'fair' and *nant* 'stream'. *See also* GWENNANT.

Gwenda f
Derived from *gwen* meaning 'fair' or 'blessed' and *da* meaning 'good'.

Gwenddoleu *m*
A hero who appears in a number of references in the earliest Welsh literature.

Gwenddydd *f*
The legendary sister of MYRDDIN (Merlin); also a saint and daughter of BRYCHAN celebrated at *Capel Gwenddydd* in Nevern.

Gwendolen, Gwendolyn *f*
Probably feminine variants of GWENDDOLEU.

Gwendraeth *f*
A river name in Carmarthenshire.

Gweneira *f*
From the Welsh *gwen* meaning 'white' and *eira* meaning 'snow', it means Snow White.

Gweneth *f*
A cross between GWYNETH and GWENITH. Gweneth Lilly is a writer of historical novels and fantasies for children.

Gwenfair *f*
A combination of *gwen* meaning 'blessed' or 'fair' and *Mair*, the Welsh for Mary.

Gwenffrwd *f*
This name has the same meaning as GWENNANT (*ffrwd* and *nant* both meaning 'stream').

Gwenfil *f*
A variant of GWENFYL.

Gwenfrewy, Gwenffrewi *f*
The saint associated with Holywell, where BEUNO restored her to life and a spring appeared where her blood had fallen. In return, she wove for him a windproof and waterproof cloak.

Gwenfyl *f*
A daughter of BRYCHAN and the saint of the former *Capel Gwenfyl* in Ceredigion.

Gwenhwyfar *f*
King ARTHUR's beautiful wife, Guinevere, whose adultery led to the ultimate downfall of the Round Table.

Gwenith *f*
The Welsh for 'wheat' but also used as a term of acclaim (*see* CIAN).

Gwenllian *f*
A heroine associated with an attack on the Norman castle of *Cydweli* in Carmarthenshire.

Gwenlyn *m*
Gwenlyn Parry was a powerful and innovative dramatist.

Gwennan *f*
A daughter of BRYCHAN. According to legend both ARTHUR and MADOG had ships of this name.

Gwennant *f*
Derived from *gwen* meaning 'fair', 'white' or 'blessed' and *nant* meaning 'stream'.

Gwenno f
An affectionate diminutive form of GWEN. Gwenno Hywyn was the author of popular children's books.

Gwenogfryn m
From the Welsh *gwenog* meaning 'favourable' or 'propitious' and *bryn* meaning 'hill'. The most famous Gwenogvryn (in its anglicised form) being Gwenogvryn Evans, a palaeographer and publisher of ancient manuscripts.

Gwent f and m
One of the old kingdoms of southeast Wales. Gwent became a county name in 1974.

Gwenyth f
A variant of GWENITH.

Gwerful, Gwerfyl f
Variants of the name of the saint celebrated in *Llanerfyl*; or as in the place name *Betws Gwerful Goch*. Gwerful Mechain is the only female poet from the Middle Ages whose work has survived. Gwerfyl Pierce Jones is the Director of the Welsh Books Council.

Gwern m
The son of BRANWEN and Matholwch, King of Ireland, in the tales of the *Mabinogion*.

Gwernydd m
A variant of GWERN.

Gwesyn m
As found in the Powys place name *Abergwesyn*.

Gwidol m
An ancient name from the third century derived from the Latin *Vitalis. See also* GWYDOL.

Gwili m
A bardic name as in the river and place name *Abergwili* in Carmarthenshire.

Gwilliam *
A surname derived from GWILYM.

Gwilym m
The English name William in Welsh. Gwilym Tell is the Welsh version of William Tell.

Gwion m
Gwion Bach (Little Gwion) was the childhood name of TALIESIN. He was the little boy who received the distilled drop of all knowledge prepared by CERIDWEN for her son AFAGDDU.

Gwladus f
Daughter of BRYCHAN, and the name of a number of characters from early Welsh history. Gwladus Ddu (black-haired) was the daughter of LLYWELYN Fawr.

Gwladys f
A variant of GWLADUS.

Gwlithen f
The Welsh for 'dewdrop'; also a

river name near Trefeca, in Powys.

Gwlithyn *m*
A masculine variant of GWLITHEN.

Gwri *m*
Gwri of the golden hair, from the tales of the *Mabinogion*.

Gwrtheyrn *m*
The Welsh form of Vortigern, a fifth-century ruler who, because of his obsession for ALIS Rhonwen, first allowed the Saxons (*Saeson*) to settle in Britain.

Gwyar *f*
A name from the early tales; she was the mother of GWALCHMAI and is also named as the wife of GERAINT, son of Erbin.

Gwyddfid *f*
The Welsh for 'honeysuckle'.

Gwyddno *m*
The legendary king of Cantre'r Gwaelod (The Drowned Hundred) who through the fecklessness of his guards, allowed his kingdom to be inundated by the sea.

Gwydion *m*
The magician son of the goddess Dôn, who created a maiden out of flowers in the tales of the *Mabinogion*. Gwydion Brooke was a well-known bassoon player.

Gwydol *m*
As found in the place name *Abergwydol* in Montgomeryshire. *See also* GWIDOL.

Gwylan *f*
A name meaning 'seagull' in English. Gwylan Thomas is the name of one of the heroines in 'the Welsh novel of the century' *Cysgod y Cryman* (The Shadow of the Sickle) by Islwyn Ffowc Ellis.

Gwylfa *m*
From *gŵyl* meaning 'feast day'.

Gwylon *m*
Another name from *gŵyl* meaning 'feast day'.

Gwyn *m*
Gwyn is a powerful adjective in Welsh meaning 'white', 'fair', 'silver', 'holy' or 'blessed'; and also a diminutive form of many of the names that follow this entry. Gwyn ap NUDD is a legendary king of the Welsh underworld. Gwyn Thomas took the south Wales mining valleys as the subject of his English novels.

Gwynallt *m*
A variant of GWENALLT.

Gwynant *m*
From *nant* meaning 'stream'. *Nant Gwynant* is a river in north Wales.

Gwyndaf *m*
An early Celtic saint. One

Gwyndaf Evans was an archdruid, another is a world-class rally driver.

Gwynedd *m*
Once a kingdom in north Wales, now a county. Ieuan Gwynedd Jones is an eminent historian.

Gwyneira *f*
A variant of GWENEIRA.

Gwyneth *f*
A feminine variant of GWYNEDD. Gwyneth Paltrow is a very successful film star.

Gwynfi *m*
Originally a river name in south Wales, which includes *gwyn* meaning 'white' or 'blessed'.

Gwynfil *m*
A parish in Ceredigion.

Gwynfor *m*
From *gwyn* meaning 'fair' or 'blessed' and *mawr* meaning 'great'. Gwynfor Evans was party leader and first Plaid Cymru Member of Parliament in 1966.

Gwynfryn *m*
A legendary place name associated with the site of the Tower of London. Hywel Gwynfryn is a popular broadcaster.

Gwynn *m*
A variant of GWYN. T Gwynn Jones was an important Welsh language poet.

Gwynno *m*
As in the parish of *Llanwynno*; he was one of the five saints of *Pumsaint* and *Llanpumsaint* (GWYN, Gwynno, GWYNORO, CEITHO and CELYNIN).

Gwynoro *m*
One of the five saints of *Pumsaint* and *Llanpumsaint* (GWYN, GWYNNO, Gwynoro, CEITHO and CELYNIN). Gwynoro Jones was a one-time Labour Member of Parliament for Carmarthenshire.

Gwyrfai *m*
A river name in GWYNEDD.

Gwyrosydd *m*
A bardic name.

Gwythyr *m*
Possibly a derivation from the Latin *Victor*. In the tale of *Culhwch ac Olwen*, he is doomed to fight GWYN ap NUDD each Calends of May until Doomsday for the beautiful CREIDDYLAD. Whoever wins on Doomsday shall gain her hand. Christine Gwyther is a Labour Assembly Member.

H

Haf *f*
The Welsh for 'summer'.

Hafgan *m*
The king of the Welsh under-world that PWYLL helped to destroy in favour of ARAWN, in the first branch of the tales from the *Mabinogion*.

Hafina *f*
A diminutive form of HAF. Hafina Clwyd is a respected journalist and broadcaster.

Hafren *f*
The Welsh for the Severn. Derived from the Latin *Sabrina*.

Hafwen *f*
Derived from HAF.

Hafwyn *m*
A masculine form of HAFWEN.

Harri, Harry *m*
From the name Henry. Harri Webb was a poet of protest and patriotism who was able to use humour to drive home his message.

Harris, Harries, Harry *
Surnames derived from HARRI.

Hawen *f*
A river name from Ceredigion.

Hawys *f*
From Hawystl, an early Celtic saint and daughter of BRYCHAN.

Hedd *m*
The Welsh for 'peace'. Hedd Wyn was the bardic name of Ellis Evans, who failed to claim the bardic chair he had won in the National Eisteddfod of 1917 as he had been killed in the Battle for Pilkem Bridge. The chair became known as 'the Black Chair of Birkenhead', a reference to the place where the Eisteddfod was held in that year.

Heddus *f*
A feminine variant derived from HEDD.

Heddwen *f*
From *hedd* meaning 'peace' and *wen* meaning 'blessed'.

Heddwyn *m*
Either a masculine version of HEDDWEN or a possibly a contraction of Hedd Wyn. *See also* HEDD.

Heddys *f*
A variant of HEDDUS.

Hedydd *m*
The Welsh for a 'skylark'.

Hefin *m*
From *haf* meaning 'summer' as in *Mehefin* (the month of June).

Hefina *f*
A feminine version of HEFIN.

Heilin *m*
A name derived from the early annals of Welsh history, possibly a son of BRYCHAN; and the saint commemorated at *Capel Heilin* in Anglesey.

Heilyn *m*
A variant of HEILIN.

Heini *m*
The Welsh for 'vigorous'; also Heinin was the chief of the twenty-four bards who served at the court of MAELGWN in the TALIESIN saga. Heini Gruffudd is a specialist in the teaching of Welsh as a second language.

Heledd *f*
A seventh-century princess of Powys, who mourns the death in battle of her brother CYNDDYLAN and all that has been lost, in a moving series of *englynion* (intricate metrical stanzas) composed in the ninth century.

Helygen *f*
The Welsh for 'willow'.

Heulfryn *m*
From *haul* meaning 'sun' and *bryn* meaning 'hill'.

Heulwen *f*
The Welsh for 'sunshine'. Heulwen Haf is a popular combination as a child's name.

Heulwyn *m*
The masculine form of HEULWEN.

Heulyn *m*
'A ray of sunshine' in English. Meinir Heulyn is a respected harpist.

Hier *
A surname derived from *hir* meaning 'tall'.

Hiraethog *m*
An administrative district in the former Denbighshire. Gwilym Hiraethog (William Rees) was dubbed in the nineteenth century as the 'father of the Welsh press'.

Hiriell *m*
A legendary hero of Gwynedd who, like ARTHUR, will awake one day to drive out the oppressors of his land.

Hopcyn *m*
From Hob, a variant of Rob, itself a diminutive form of Robert, plus the diminutive *cyn*.

Hopkins *
A surname derived from HOPCYN.

Howel *m*
A variant of HYWEL. Howel Harris was an important eighteenth-cen-

tury leader of the Methodist Revival in Wales.

Howell(s) *
A surname derived from HYWEL.

Huail *m*
The fifth-century son of Caw and a distinguished soldier who would submit to no one, not even King ARTHUR. He was finally caught and executed at Rhuddlan, where to this day there stands a stone inscribed with his name.

Hughes, Huws *
Surnames derived from HUW.

Huw *m*
It is more than likely that this is a Welsh spelling of Hugh, but it could well be in some cases a diminutive form of HYWEL when pronounced as *Hiwel*. Huw Edwards is a news anchorman and broadcaster and Huw Llewelyn Davies a respected broadcaster and rugby commentator.

Hwfa *m*
A bardic name associated with the place name *Trehwfa* in Anglesey; also an early heroic name.

Hwlcyn *m*
An affectionate diminutive form of HYWEL.

Hyfaidd *m*
A heroic name from the earliest Welsh poetry – 'a warrior whose valour should be praised while there are minstrels to do so.'

Hywel *m*
A name from early Welsh history, associated especially with the tenth-century codifier of Welsh law, Hywel Dda, king of all Wales except Gwent and Morgannwg.

Hywyn *m*
The saint of Aberdaron in Gwynedd. John Hywyn is a contemporary poet.

I

Iago *m*
The name James in Welsh. Iago Prytherch is a character created by the poet R S Thomas.

Ianto *m*
An affectionate diminutive of IFAN or IEUAN. Ianto Full Pelt was a popular nickname.

Idloes *m*
The sixth-century saint commemorated in the place name *Llanidloes*.

Idris *m*
The legendary giant who used the mountain, *Cader Idris*, as his seat (*cadair*). Idris Reynolds is a contemporary Welsh language poet

who composes in traditional strict metres.

Idwal *m*
A name that appears frequently in the early history of Wales. One Idwal Jones was a Cardiganshire writer who did not believe the Welsh took their humour seriously enough; another created the popular detective Gari Tryfan.

Iestyn *m*
The Welsh for Justin; and the saint commemorated in the place name *Llaniestyn*.

Ieuan *m*
A Welsh version of Iohannes and the name of several early saints. Ieuan Evans is a one-time captain of the Welsh rugby team. See also IOAN.

Ifan *m*
A variant of IEUAN. Ifan ab Owen Edwards was the founder of the Welsh youth movement, the Urdd.

Ifanna *f*
A feminine version of IFAN.

Ifor *m*
A name from the early annals of Welsh history, possibly a diminutive form of CADIFOR. Ifor Bach was a twelfth-century lord of Senghennydd who successfully attacked Cardiff Castle and captured William Earl of Gloucester, his wife and his son. He released them on having his lands restored. Ifor ap Glyn is a poet who bridges the world of pop song and classical poetry.

Ilid *f*
An early Celtic saint as commemorated at *Llanilid* in the Vale of Glamorgan; mother of CURIG.

Illtud *m*
An early warrior turned Celtic saint. Greatly respected as one of the most learned men of his day, he established a seat of learning at *Llanilltud Fawr* (Llantwit Major) in the Vale of Glamorgan.

Illtyd *m*
A variant of ILLTUD. Illtyd Harrington was a prominent London politician.

Ina *f*
The daughter of CEREDIG; and the saint commemorated at *Llanina* in Ceredigion.

Indeg *f*
One of the ladies of King ARTHUR's court and a standard of beauty for the poets.

Ioan *m*
From the Latin *Iohannes* (the Biblical John). Ioan Bowen Rees was an authority on constitutional matters and a keen mountaineer. See also IEUAN.

Iola *f*
A feminine form of IOLO. Iola

Gregory is a popular and accomplished actress.

Iolo m
A diminutive form of IORWERTH. Iolo Morganwg was an antiquary, a scholar, a forger and the creator of the Eisteddfodic Gorsedd of Bards.

Ion m
From *Ionawr* (January).

Iona f
From *Ionawr* (January).

Iorwerth m
A name that appears in the early genealogies of the kings of Powys. Iorwerth Cyfeiliog Peate was a man of letters and the creator and first curator of the Folk Museum at St Fagans.

Irfon m
A river name in Powys associated with the death of LLYWELYN, the last independent Prince of Wales

Irwen f
A feminine variant of IRWYN.

Irwyn m
From *ir* meaning 'fresh' or 'vigorous' and *gwyn* meaning 'blessed'. Irwyn Walters was the driving spirit behind the formation of the National Youth Orchestra of Wales.

Isfoel m
The bardic name of Dafydd Jones, one of the Cilie family of poets from Ceredigion.

Isfryn m
A bardic name taken from place names.

Islwyn m
A Gwent place name from *is* meaning 'below' and *llwyn* meaning 'grove'; it was taken as a bardic name by one William Thomas who wrote with passion about love and religion.

Ithel m
A name from the early annals associated with Gwent and Glamorgan.

Iwan m
A variant of IFAN. Daydd Iwan is a modern balladeer and composer of classic songs of love and protest.

J

Jones *
A surname derived from John via the Welsh version, Siôn.

K

(There is no letter 'K' in the Welsh alphabet.)

Keidrych *m*
An anglicised form of CEIDRYCH.
Keidrych Rhys was an Anglo-
Welsh author and editor.

Kemys *
A surname from the place name
Cemais.

Kendrick *
A surname from CYNFRIG or
Cynwrig. However, the name could
also have Irish origins.

Kenfyn *m*
A name derived from CYNFYN.

Kenwyn *m*
A name derived from CYNFYN.

Kyffin *m*
An anglicised form of CYFFIN.
Sir Kyffin Williams is recog-
nised as being among the most
important of contemporary
Welsh painters.

L

Leri *f*
A diminutive form of ELERI, TELERI
and MELERI.

Lewis *
From the French *Louis*. This is the
name the medieval clerks substituted
for Llewelyn (LLYWELYN) and eventually it replaced Llewelyn as the
official name used in documents.

Lili *f*
The Welsh word for a 'lily'.

Lilwen *f*
Derived from LILI and *wen* meaning 'white' or fair'.

Lisa *f*
A diminutive of Elisabeth. 'Lisa
Lân' is the title of a well-known
folk song.

Llefelys *m*
A name from the tales of *Lludd a
Llefelys* in the *Mabinogion*, where
he becomes, through marriage,
King of France.

Lleu, Llew *m*
The Celtic god of light for whom
BLODEUWEDD was created as a wife
from the flowers of the oak, the
broom and the meadowsweet – as
told in the tales of the *Mabinogion*.

Lleucu f
An early Celtic saint celebrated at *Betws Leucu* in Ceredigion; and the Welsh equivalent of Lucy. The death of Lleucu Llwyd was the subject of a moving twelfth-century poem and a twentieth-century pop song.

Lleufer m
A name meaning 'light'. Lleufer Mawr (Great Light) was an epithet given to one of the early kings of Britain. Daniel Lleufer Thomas was an important figure in educational reform at the beginning of the twentieth century.

Llew m
An affectionate diminutive form of LLEWELYN and a variant of LLEU; also the Welsh word for a 'lion'.

Llewela f
A variant of LLYWELA.

Llewelyn m
A variant of LLYWELYN.

Llian f
The Welsh for 'linen'; and also a diminutive of GWENLLIAN [Gwenllïan] and a variant of LLUAN.

Llifon m
A river name from Gwynedd.

Llinos f
The Welsh for a 'linnet'.

Llio f
An affectionate diminutive form of GWENLLÏAN. Llio Millward is a popular singer and entertainer.

Llion m
Llion Gawr (the Giant) was one of twenty-four mighty kings, and tradition claims that *Caerllion* (Caerleon-on-Usk) is located where Llion had his castle.

Lloyd m *
A forename and surname derived from LLWYD. David Lloyd was a Welsh tenor whose recordings remain popular.

Lluan f
A daughter of BRYCHAN and the name found in the place name *Llanlluan* in Carmarthenshire.

Lludd m
A legendary king of Britain whose tale is told in *Lludd a Llefelys* in the tales of the *Mabinogion*.

Llwyd m
The Welsh for 'grey' and 'holy'. Morgan Llwyd was a leading Welsh Puritan during the seventeenth century. *See* LLOYD.

Llŷr m
A name from early Welsh legend which became Lear in English. Brychan Llŷr has been a lead singer with a number of Welsh pop groups. Leicester is known as *Caerlŷr* (Llŷr's fortress) in Welsh.

Llywarch *m*
A frequently occurring name in the early Welsh annals. Llywarch Hen is the subject of a series of ninth-century poems mourning the loss of his twenty-four sons who were killed in battle while defending their father's land.

Llywela *f*
A feminine variant of LLYWELYN.

Llywelyn *m*
A prominent name in the genealogies of the kings and princes of Wales. Llywelyn ap Iorwerth or Llywelyn Fawr (the Great) was the greatest of the Welsh rulers of the Middle Ages.

Lona *f*
A diminutive form of MOELONA. *Lona* was the title of a novel by the poet T Gwynn Jones.

Lowri *f*
The Welsh form of the name Laura.

Luc *m*
The Welsh form of the Biblical Luke.

Luned *f*
A variant of ELUNED. *Luned Bengoch* (Redhead) is the title of a novel which has appealed to generations of children.

Lyn, Lynn *m*
A diminutive form of LLYWELYN. Lynn Davies won a gold medal in the long jump in the 1964 Tokyo Olympics.

Lyn, Lynne *f*
A diminutive form of ELUNED, LUNED.

Lynwen *f*
Lyn with the addition of the suffix *wen* meaning 'fair'.

M

Mabli *f*
The Welsh for Mabel.

Mabon *m*
The Celtic god of youth; and the bardic name of William Abraham, a Rhondda Member of Parliament and miners' leader.

Machreth *m*
A bardic name. The saint commemo-

rated at *Llanfachreth* in Anglesey.

Macsen *m*
Macsen Wledig is the Welsh name of Magnus Maximus who was proclaimed Roman Emperor by the armed troops under his command in Britain in AD 383.

Madlen *f*
The Welsh form of Magdalene.

Madoc *m*
A variant of MADOG.

Madog *m*
A name that appears frequently in the early histories, the most famous being the twelfth-century Prince of Gwynedd to whom is attributed the discovery of America.

Mael *m*
An early Celtic saint and popular genealogical name.

Maelgwn, Maelgwyn *m*
A powerful ruler of sixth-century Britain, associated with present day Gwynedd.

Maelor *m*
An administrative district of the former Flintshire; also the name of a giant who lived at *Castell Maelor* above Aberystwyth.

Mai *f*
The Welsh for 'May'.

Mair *f*
A Welsh form of Mary.

Mairwen *f*
From MAIR and *wen* meaning 'blessed'; it could also be a variant of MARWENNA.

Mal *m*
A diminutive form of MALDWYN. Mal Pope is a popular entertainer.

Maldwyn *m*
From the Norman name Baldwin, as found in the place name *Trefaldwyn* (Montgomery).

Malen *f*
From Magdalene.

Mali *f*
The Welsh equivalent of Molly. 'Sali Mali' is a popular character in books for young children.

Mallt *f*
The Welsh equivalent of Matilda or Maud.

Manawydan *m*
One of the immortals who is the subject of the fourth branch of the tales of the *Mabinogion*. The Welsh name for the Isle of Man is *Ynys Manaw* which is probably derived from Manawydan.

Manod *f and m*
The name of a mountain in Merioneth and a lake in Ceredigion.

Manon *f*
An old Welsh word for 'queen'. Manon Rhys is a popular novelist and scriptwriter.

Marc *m*
The Welsh form of the Biblical Mark.

March *m*
The King Mark of the Trystan leg-

end, husband of ESYLLT. *March* is also the Welsh for 'stallion' and, according to Welsh tradition, King March had the ears of a horse which no one but his barber knew about.

Mared f
A variant of MERERID.

Maredudd m
A noble name from the early annals.

Marged f
The Welsh form of Margaret.

Margiad f
The north Wales form of MARGED.

Mari f
A Welsh form of Mary.

Marlais m
A Carmarthenshire river name and the middle name of the poet Dylan Thomas.

Marles m
Derived from MARLAIS.

Marwenna f
A Celtic saint and daughter of BRYCHAN associated with churches in Cornwall.

Math m
The wizard King of Gwynedd found in the tales of the *Mabinogion*.

Mathonwy m
The name of the father of MATH.

Mati f
A diminutive form of MARGED.

Mayler *
A surname derived from MEILYR.

Mayne *
A surname derived from *main* meaning 'thin'.

Mechain m
An administrative district in the old kingdom of Powys. Gwallter Mechain was the bardic name of an early nineteenth-century editor and poet.

Medi f
The Welsh for 'September'.

Medrod m
An exemplary warrior in the early Welsh tradition, but not such a shining knight by the time he reaches the Arthurian legends.

Medwen f
A feminine variant form of MEDWYN.

Medwyn m
An early Celtic saint; there is also a legendary Medwin.

Megan f
A diminutive Welsh form of Meg, itself a diminutive form of Margaret. Megan Lloyd George was the politician daughter of David Lloyd George.

Mei *m*
A diminutive form of MEILIR and MEIRION.

Meic *m*
Normally a Welsh version of Mike. However, early Welsh legend boasted a Meic Myngfras (Shaggy-haired Meic) and the name appears in early genealogies. Meic Stephens is a poet, critic and anthologist who has compiled a book of Welsh names for children.

Meidrym *m*
A place name from Carmarthenshire.

Meilir *m*
An early Celtic saint as found in the place name *Trefeilyr*.

Meilyr *m*
A variant of MEILIR.

Meinir *f*
A Welsh word for 'maiden'. Meinir Pierce Jones is an author and scriptwriter.

Meinwen *f*
A Welsh word for a 'maiden'.

Meirion *m*
A grandson of Cunedda, a dynastic ruler of northern Britain, many of whose sons and grandsons became saints or rulers who gave their names to old Welsh kingdoms. Meirion gave his name to *Meirionnydd* (Merioneth).

Meirwen *f*
A variant of MAIRWEN.

Meirwyn *m*
A masculine variant of MEIRWEN.

Melangell *f*
The patron saint of hares, which are known in Welsh as, *Ŵyn Melangell* (Melangell's lambs).

Meleri *f*
The wife of CEREDIG and St David's grandmother.

Mellen, Mellings *
Surnames derived from *melyn* meaning 'yellow (haired)'.

Melwas *m*
Melwas was a standard for accomplishment in early Welsh tradition but a traitor by the time he reached the Welsh Arthurian legend.

Men *f*
A diminutive form of MENNA.

Menai *f*
An ancient name of Celtic origin as found in the Menai Straits that divide Anglesey from the mainland.

Menna *f*
A name made popular by the nineteenth-century Welsh poet, John Ceiriog Hughes, in his poem 'Alun Mabon'. Menna Elfyn is a highly respected poet and novelist.

Merêd *m*
A diminutive form of MEREDYDD.

Meredith *
A surname derived from MEREDYDD.

Meredydd *m*
A variant of MAREDUDD. Meredydd Evans is a philosopher, musician and tireless campaigner for the Welsh language.

Mererid *f*
From the Latin *margarita*, which is derived from the Greek word meaning a 'pearl'.

Merfyn *m*
A name from the early Welsh genealogies.

Meriadoc *m*
An early Celtic saint associated with Cornwall and Brittany though maybe of Welsh origin.

Merierid *f*
A variant of MERERID.

Merrick *
A surname from MEURIG.

Mervyn *m*
The anglicised form of MERFYN. Mervyn Burch is a composer and Mervyn Davies played at Number 8 for Wales and the British Lions.

Meurig *m*
A frequent name in the early genealogies and found in the place name *Trefeurig* in Ceredigion.

Meuryn *m*
A bardic name.

Meyrick *
A surname from MEURIG.

Miall *m*
A *nom de plume* created by Twm Miall, the author of racy contemporary stories.

Mihangel *m*
A compression of Michael Archangel as in the many *Llanfihangel* place names which have churches dedicated to St Michael. Mihangel Morgan is a contemporary story writer and literary critic.

Milwyn *m*
A reversal of the elements in GWYNFIL.

Mirain *f*
The Welsh for 'fair', 'comely' or 'refined'.

Moc *m*
A diminutive form of MORGAN.

Modlen *f*
An affectionate variant of MADLEN.

Moelona *f*
Originally the *nom de plume* of a popular author who took the name from the name of the farm where she lived (*Moylon* from *moel* '

bare' or 'bald'). The diminutive form LONA has come into popular use in recent years.

Moelwen *f*
A feminine variant of MOELWYN.

Moelwyn *m*
A mountain in north Wales, from *moel* 'bald' and *gwyn* 'white'. It could be a variant of MAELGWYN.

Môn *m*
The Welsh word for Anglesey.

Mona *f*
A feminine form of MÔN.

Mordaf *m*
Together with NUDD and RHYDDERCH, one of 'the Three Generous Men of the Isles of Britain'.

Morfudd *f*
The fair-haired beauty who inspired the great Welsh poet, Dafydd ap Gwilym; and a twin sister to OWAIN. Morfudd Llwyn Owen was an accomplished composer who died at a tragically early age.

Morgan *m* *
A frequent name in the early genealogies and found in *Morgannwg* (Glamorgan). Rhodri Morgan is the First Minister of the Welsh National Assembly.

Morien *m*
A heroic name from the early an-

nals and genealogies; and the pen name of a journalist who supported the cause of the miners in the early twentieth century.

Morlais *m*
A tenth-century bishop of Bangor and river name in Carmarthenshire.

Morris *m* *
A forename and surname which is a variant of MORYS.

Morwenna *f*
From *morwyn* 'maid' or 'virgin'; an early Celtic saint and daughter of BRYCHAN.

Morys *m*
From the Latin *Mauricius*, which also gave MEURIG.

Mostyn *m*
As in the village of Mostyn near Flint.

Myfanwy *f*
A historic name made popular by the song of the same name by Joseph Parry.

Myfi *f*
A diminutive form of MYFANWY.

Myfyr *m*
As in the place name *Llanfihangel Glyn Myfyr*, similar to *myfyriwr* meaning 'student' but more likely to be from an old Welsh word for 'grave'.

Myrddin *m*
Known in English as Merlin. Falsely derived from the place name *Caerfyrddin* (Carmarthen). Myrddin ap Dafydd is a popular contemporary poet who became the 'Children's Poet Laureate' during the year 2000.

Myrdeg *f*
A name incorporating *teg* meaning 'fair'.

N

Nanney *
A surname from *nanneu*, a plural form of *nant* 'stream'.

Nanno *f*
An affectionate diminutive of Ann.

Nantlais *m*
A bardic name. William Nantlais Williams was a popular lyric poet and composer of hymns.

Nedw *m*
A diminutive affectionate form of Ned.

Nefydd *m*
Traditionally the saint celebrated in the place name *Llanefydd* but likely to have been wrongly ascribed.

Neifion *m*
The Welsh equivalent of Neptune.

Nerys *f*
Feminine form from *nêr* meaning 'lord' or possibly a diminutive form of Generys. Nerys Hughes is a popular actress and television personality.

Nest *f*
A Welsh affectionate diminutive form of Agnes, a name from early Welsh history derived from the Greek word for 'pure'. Nest, the daughter of Rhys ap TEWDWR, was a renowned beauty who took many lovers, one of whom was Henry I.

Nesta *f*
A variant of NEST.

Nia *f*
An Irish name made popular in Wales by the poet T Gwynn Jones.

Ninian *m*
A famous early Celtic saint associated with the conversion of the Picts in what is now Scotland. Ninian Park is the home of Cardiff City Football Club.

Non *f*
The mother of St David.

Nona *f*
A variant of NON.

Now *m*
The north Wales diminutive form of Owen.

Nudd *m*
Celebrated by the poets as one of the 'Three Generous Men of the Isle of Britain'.

Nye *m*
The diminutive form of Aneirin or Aneurin as in Nye Bevan.

O

Odwyn *m*
As found in the place name *Llanbadarn Odwyn* in Ceredigion, which has legendary connections with a giant of this name.

Ogwen *m*
A river name in Gwynedd, from Ogfanw, a very old form (possibly an old goddess). John Ogwen is an actor and broadcaster.

Olwen *f*
The beautiful heroine of the tale of *Culhwch ac Olwen* – white clover grew where she walked. 'The Dream of Olwen' is a popular piece of music for piano.

Olwenna *f*
A variant of Olwen.

Onllwyn *m*
As in the place name in the Dulais Valley. Onllwyn Brace was a well-known rugby player.

Oriel *m*
The Welsh word for 'gallery'.

Orig *m*
A variant of Orwig. Orig Willams is a former heavy-weight wrestler.

Orwig *m*
The personal name that follows *din* (an ancient word for 'fortress') in the village of *Dinorwig* in Gwynedd.

Osian *m*
A poet of Irish legend. Osian Ellis is a harpist for whom many contemporary composers have written works.

Oswallt *m*
The Welsh equivalent of Oswald. *Croes* (cross) *Oswallt* is the Welsh for Oswestry.

Owain *m*
A name that goes back to the earliest legends and genealogies. Owain Arwel Hughes is a well-known classical conductor.

Owen *m*
A variant of Owain.

Owena *f*
A feminine form of Owain.

P

Padarn *m*
A name from fourth-century British Roman times and also the saint celebrated at *Llanbadarn* in Ceredigion.

Parry *
A surname derived from ap Harri.

Pedr *m*
The Welsh equivalent of Peter.

Pedrog *m*
A fifth-century Celtic saint commemorated in the place name *Llanbedrog*, though he would seem to be more strongly associated with Cornwall. In Welsh tradition, he was one of the seven warriors to escape unscathed from Arthur's last battle at Camlan.

Pennant *m*
As in the place name *Cwm Pennant*. Richard Pennant, Lord Penrhyn, was a nineteenth-century slate magnate.

Pennar *m*
As in the place name *Aberpennar* (Mountain Ash) from *pennardd* 'highlands'. Pennar Davies was a highly regarded literary figure.

Penrhyn *m*
A place name as in *Penrhyndeudraeth* meaning 'headland'.

Penri *m*
From ap Henri, the Welsh form of Henry.

Penry *
A surname variant of Penri. John Penry was a Puritan martyr.

Peredur *m*
A knight and hero of Arthurian romances.

Peris *m*
A river name as found in *Llanberis*.

Povey *
A surname derived from ap Hwfa.

Powell *
A surname derived from ap Hywel.

Powys *m*
An ancient Welsh kingdom and modern Welsh county.

Preece, Price *
Surnames derived from ap Rhys.

Prichard, Pritchard *
Surnames derived from ap Rhisiart.

Probert *
A surname derived from ap Robert, the English form of the Welsh Robat.

Prosser *
A surname derived from ap
RHOSIER.

Prothero, Prydderch *
Surnames derived from ap
RHYDDERCH.

Pryderi *m*
The name of the original subject
of the tales of the *Mabinogion*.

Prydwen *f*
A forename from *pryd* 'complexion' and *wen* 'fair' or 'white'.

Prys *m*
A forename from an old place
name and a variant of *prysg* meaning 'copse' or 'thicket'. Also from
ap RHYS. Prys Edwards was a
Chairman of S4C and the Welsh
Tourist Board.

Prysor *m*
The name of a stream popularised
in a famous Welsh poem.

Prytherch *
Another surname variant of
PRYDDERCH.

Puw, Pughe *
Surnames derived from ap HUW.

Pwyll *m*
The legendary Prince of DYFED
who appears in the tales of the
Mabinogion. *Pwyll* is also the
Welsh word for 'caution'.

R

Rebeca *f*
A Biblical name. This was the
name taken by a group of men who
dressed up as women to destroy the
toll-gates in southwest Wales in the
nineteenth century. *See also* BECA.

Rees *
A surname from RHYS.

Rheinallt *m*
The Welsh form of Reynold or its
later forms, Reginald or Ronald.

Rhian *f*
A variant of RHIAIN.

Rhiain *f*
The Welsh for a maiden.

Rhianedd, Rhianydd *f*
Variants derived from RHIAIN.

Rhiannon *f*
A Celtic goddess who appears in
the tales of the *Mabinogion*.
Rhiannon is the name of a contemporary craftswoman working in
gold and silver.

Rhianwen *f*
A variant of RHIAIN; also from *wen*
meaning 'fair' or blessed'.

Rhidian *m*
The saint's name found in *Llanrhidian,*
but probably wrongly ascribed.

Rhion *m*
From *rhi*, an old word for 'king'.

Rhisiart *m*
The Welsh for Richard.

Rhodri *m*
A name which frequently appears in
early legend and genealogies. Rhodri
Morgan is the current First Minister
of the National Assembly of Wales.

Rholant *m*
Roland, the hero famous for his
friendship with Oliver in the Charlemagne tales. *See also Rolant.*

Rhona *f*
A diminutive form of RHONWEN.

Rhonabwy *m*
The hero of the Arthurian romance
Breuddwyd Rhonabwy (The
Dream of Rhonabwy).

Rhonwen *f*
The Welsh form of Rowena. Alis
Rhonwen was the beautiful daughter of Hengist, 'mother of the English'. *See also* ALIS.

Rhosier *m*
The Welsh form of Roger.

Rhoslyn *m*
From *rhos* meaning 'moor' and
llyn meaning 'lake'.

Rhoswen *f*
The Welsh for 'fair rose'.

Rhun *m*
The name of one of 'the Three Fair
Princes of the Isles of Britain'.

Rhydderch *m*
A forename that originally meant
'ruddy' or 'reddish brown'.
Rhydderch was one of 'the Three
Generous Men of the Isle of Brit-
ain'.

Rhydian *m*
A variant of RHIDIAN.

Rhydwen *m*
From a place name, perhaps from
rhyd meaning 'ford' and *wen*
meaning 'holy'. Rhydwen
Williams was a poet, broadcaster
and novelist of the south Wales
mining community.

Rhys *m*
A frequently occurring name in the
early pedigrees and genealogies,
from *rhys* meaning 'hero'. Yr
Arglwydd Rhys (The Lord Rhys)
is accredited with holding the first
eisteddfod-type competition at Cardigan in 1176. Rhys Ifans is a contemporary actor and film star.

Rhystud *m*
The sixth-century saint of
Llanrhystud in Ceredigion.

Rian *f*
A variant of RHIAN.

Robat *m*
The Welsh for Robert. Robat Powell is a Welsh learner who is a master of the traditional Welsh strict poetic metres. Robat Gruffudd is the head of the Lolfa publishing house.

Rol *m*
A diminutive form of ROLANT.

Rolant *m*
The Welsh form of Roland, the hero famed for his friendship with Oliver in the Charlemagne cycle of tales. *See also* Rholant.

Ronw *m*
A variant of GRONW.

Ronwen *f*
A variant of RHONWEN.

Rosser *
A surname derived from RHOSIER.

S

Sandde *m*
A warrior with the face of an angel who is said to have escaped from ARTHUR's last battle owing to his beauty.

Sara *f*
A girl's name from the Biblical Sarah.

Seimon *m*
A boy's name from the Biblical Simon.

Seiriol *m*
The sixth-century Celtic saint of *Ynys Seiriol* (Puffin Island). According to tradition, Seiriol faced west in the morning and east in the evening and, by so doing, he preserved his fair complexion and was known as Seiriol Wyn (Fair Seiriol). *See also* CYBI.

Seisyll *m*
From the Latin name *Sextilius*. *See also* CECIL.

Selyf *m*
The Welsh for Solomon.

Seren *f*
The Welsh for 'star'.

Shan, Shân, Shani *f*
Variants of SIÂN.

Shon, Shôn, Shoni *m*
Variants of SIÔN.

Siams *m*
The Welsh form of James.

Siân, Sian *f*
The Welsh form of Jane. Siân Phillips is an actress in both Welsh and English and an international

film star. Siân Edwards is a conductor of classical music.

Sianco *m*
A diminutive form of SIENCYN.

Siani *f*
A diminutive form of SIÂN.

Siarl *m*
The Welsh form of Charles.

Sieffre *m*
The Welsh form of Geoffrey. Sieffre o Fynwy (Geoffrey of Monmouth) was the author of the important twelfth-century *History of the Kings of Britain.*

Siencyn *m*
The Welsh form of Jenkin.

Silyn *m*
A saint's name from the Middle Ages as in the place name *Cwm Silyn* in Gwynedd.

Simwnt *m*
The Welsh form of Simon.

Siôn *m*
The Welsh form of John.

Sioned *f*
The Welsh form of Janet or a feminine form of SIÔN.

Sioni *m*
The south Wales diminutive of SIÔN.

Sionyn *m*
The north Wales diminutive of SIÔN.

Siôr *m*
The Welsh form of George.

Siriol *f*
The Welsh for 'happy' or 'content'.

Siwan *f*
The Welsh for Joan. The most famous Siwan was the thirteenth-century wife of LLYWELYN Fawr and the subject of the drama *Siwan* by Saunders Lewis.

Steffan *m*
The Welsh for Stephen, as found in the place name *Llansteffan*. *San Steffan* is the Welsh for Westminster and *Gŵyl San Steffan* is the Welsh for Boxing Day.

Styfin *m*
A variant of STEFFAN.

Sulien *m*
An early saint and 11th-century bishop of St David's.

Sulwen *f*
The daughter of GERAINT according to one source.

Sulwyn *m*
Masculine form of SULWEN. Sulwyn Thomas is a popular broadcaster.

T

Taffy *m*
The eponymous Welshman like
Jock from Scotland and Paddy
from Ireland. Probably a conven-
ient mix of *Dafi* (Davy) from
DAFYDD and the River Taff that
flows through Cardiff.

Talfan *m*
Possibly a variant of Talafan, an
ancient administrative region in
South Wales.

Talfryn *m*
Made up of the two elements *tal*
meaning 'high' and *bryn* meaning
'hill'.

Talhaearn *m*
The name of one of the earliest
Welsh poets dubbed 'father of poetic art' who composed in the sixth
century; also a bardic name derived
from the village name *Llanfair
Talhaearn*.

Taliesin *m*
The name of one of the earliest
Welsh poets whose work has
survived; also the hero of *The
Tale of Taliesin* which tells how
little GWION (the childhood
name of Taliesin) inadvertently
becomes the wisest man in the
world through the sorcery of
CERIDWEN.

Tanwen *f*
A name made up of *tân* meaning
'flame' or 'fire' and *wen* meaning
'pure'.

Taran *m*
The Welsh for 'a peal of thunder';
also a legendary name.

Tathan *f*
The saint commemorated in the
place name *St (T)athan. See also*
DATHAN.

Tawe *m*
A river name as in *Abertawe*
(Swansea).

Tecwyn *m*
An early saint commemorated at
Llandecwyn in Merioneth. Tecwyn
Lloyd was a man of letters and
practical joker.

Tegau *f*
The name of an early heroine
famed for her beauty and fidelity.

Tegerin *m*
An ancestor of two tribes in Anglesey.

Tegid *m*
As in *Llyn Tegid* (Bala Lake); also
the husband of CERIDWEN in *The
Tale of Taliesin*.

Tegla *m*
The saint commemorated in *Llandegla* in Denbighshire. Tegla Davies was a minister and religious writer during the first half of the twentieth century.

Tegryn *m*
A forename after the village of the same name in Ceredigion.

Tegwedd *f*
From *teg* meaning 'fair' and *gwedd* meaning 'form'.

Tegwel *m*
A variant of DEGWEL.

Tegwen *f*
The eminine form of TEGWYN.

Tegwyn *m*
A variant if TECWYN.

Teifi *m*
A river name as in the town *Aberteifi* (Cardigan). Hywel Teifi Edwards is a popular historian, broadcaster and man of letters.

Teifion *m*
A variant of EIFION.

Teifryn *m*
A combination of TEIFI and *bryn,* meaning 'hill'.

Teilo *m*
An important fifth-century saint with many churches dedicated to his name, the most important being at *Llandeilo.*

Teleri *f*
A variant of ELERI. Teleri Bevan was an important broadcaster and head of programmes at the BBC.

Telor *f* and *m*
A Welsh word meaning 'singer'.

Terfel *m*
A variant of DERFEL. The internationally acclaimed opera singer Bryn Terfel is the most famous person of this name.

Terwyn *m*
A word meaning 'brilliant', 'fierce' or 'ardent'.

Tewdwr *m*
A popular early name which eventually became anglicised as Tudor. A royal name long associated with Anglesey.

Teyrnon *m*
From *teyrn* 'lord' or 'ruler'; a legendary figure who appears in the tales of the *Mabinogion.*

Tomos *m*
The Welsh masculine form of Thomas.

Tonwen, Tonwenna *f*
Two forms of the name of the wife of the legendary British king, DYFNWAL Moelmud.

Towy *m*
A variant of TYWI.

Towyn *m*
A variant of TYWYN.

Trahaearn *m*
A name from early legend, the fictitious father of MACSEN.

Trebor *m*
An anagram. The bardic name *Trebor Mai* is 'I am Robert' backwards.

Trefin *m*
A bardic name after the village of that name in Pembrokeshire.

Trefina *f*
The feminine form of TREFIN.

Trefor *m*
Originally a place name from *tref* 'town' or 'stead' and *fawr* 'large'. Its use as a family name has been traced back to the place of that name in the parish of Llangollen.

Treharne *
A surname derived from TRAHAEARN.

Trevor *
A surname derived from TREFOR.

Tristan *m*
A variant of TRYSTAN.

Tryfan *m*
A mountain in Gwynedd. Gari

Tryfan was a popular fictitious detective.

Trystan *m*
Possibly a Pictish name borrowed by the Welsh but made popular in the tale of *Trystan ac Esyllt* (Tristan and Isolde).

Tudfil *f*
A variant of TUDFUL.

Tudfor *m*
From the place name *Cwmtudu* on the coast of Ceredigion, and consisting of *tud* meaning 'land', and *môr* meaning 'sea'. Tudfor Jones was a popular poet with a wild streak of humour.

Tudful, Tudfyl *f*
Names derived from the saint of *Merthyr Tudful*.

Tudno *m*
From the saint of *Llandudno*.

Tudor *m* *
From TUDUR.

Tudur *m* *
From an old Celtic form *Teutorix* made up of 'tribe' and 'king'; an early Celtic saint and an important figure in the early genealogies. Henry Tudor is known as Harri Tudur in Welsh. A Welsh masculine form of Theodore.

Tudwal *m*
As in *Tudweiliog* (the land of

Tudwal) in Llŷn; also an early Celtic saint.

T(y)weli *m*
From a river name in Carmarthenshire. Tweli Griffiths is a well-known broadcaster.

Twm *m*
A diminutive form of TOMOS. Twm Siôn Cati was a historical figure who became 'the wild wag of Wales' in stories.

Twynog *m*
From *twyn* meaning 'hillock' or 'dune'.

Tydai *m*
A legendary early Welsh poet.

Tydfil *f*
A variant of TUDFUL.

Tydfor *m*
A variant of TUDFOR.

Tyleri *f*
As found in the place name *Abertyleri*; a variant of TELERI.

Tysul *m*
The fifth-century saint of *Llandysul*.

Tywi *m*
A river name in Carmarthenshire.

Tywyn *m*
A Gwynedd place name.

U

Uchdryd *m*
The name of a red-bearded hero from Arthurian romance; and as found in the place name *Hafod Uchdryd* in Ceredigion.

Urien *m*
A lord of the Britons famed for his valour. Urien Wiliam is a language specialist and writer of mystery stories.

V

(There is no V in the Welsh alphabet.)

Vaughan *m* *
A forename and surname derived from *bychan* meaning 'small'. *See also* FYCHAN.

Voyle *
A surname from *moel* meaning 'bald'.

W

Wenna *f*
A diminutive form of AWENA and MORWENA.

Williams *
A surname based on GWILYM or William.

Winston *m* *
A forename or surname from *tref* meaning 'town' or 'ton' and 'win' a variant of GWYN or WYN (*trefwyn* means Wyn's town).

Worgan *
A surname that could be derived from Gwrgan, an ancient dynastic name of kings from the Middle Ages which has fallen into disuse.

Wyn, Wynn *m*
Variants of GWYN.

Wyre *m*
A Ceredigion river name. Wyre Davies is a broadcaster.

Y

Ynyr *m*
A forename taken from the Latin *Honorius*.

Ywain *m*
A variant of OWAIN.

The Nicknames of Ynys-y-bŵl

(As recalled by Jonathan Thomas and Johnny Morgan
and recorded by Sarah Ann Thomas)

Shoni Aberdâr
John from Aberdare

Glyn Acid
Glyn was responsible for checking
the acid in the batteries of the elec-
tric lamps used underground by the
miners.

Ianto'r Allt-ddu
Evan from Allt-ddu

George Apollos
George was a keep-fit fanatic who
kept himself in good shape.

Twm yr Asgwrn
Thomas the Bone

John Bachan Budur
John Bit of a Lad

Mari Back Kitchen

John Baco'r Nef
John Heavenly 'Bacco

Tommy Bacon

John Bad English
John wanted to visit his daughter
who had had a baby. When he ar-
rived at the station, he said 'I want
a ticket for she and me back and
front (a return).' 'Where to?' asked
the clerk. 'Mind your business.'
came the reply. 'My daughter
marry "Glasshouse Bobby" (a rail-
way signalman).'

Dai Baltic
Baltic was the name of a coal seam
in the Lady Windsor Colliery.

Dai Bandy
Bow-legged Dai

Dai Bara Bwngy
Dai was built like a cottage loaf,
square and stocky.

Wil Bara-jam
Wil Bread and Jam

Mrs Jones Bara Menyn
Mrs Jones Bread and Butter. The
tale is told elsewhere of a stranger

asking a villager 'Could you tell me where I could find David Jones?' There were so many David Joneses, that the villager didn't know where to begin. 'I believe he's called Dai Bara Menyn,' said the stranger. 'Oh, that's me!' came the reply, 'What can I do for you?'

Shoni Ben Pwll
Johnny Top Pit (i.e. the part above ground)

Wil Better Mate

Jack Black

Dai Blinker
Dai suffered from a tremorous eyelid.

Dai Bobby

Bili Bomper
Bili drove a locomotive with bumpers.

Shoni Bouncer

Dai Bricko
Dai lived in one of the first houses to be built with bricks round the door (known locally as the 'Brickhouses').

Tom Davies Bristol

Wil Bron Sythu
Wil I'm Freezing

Charlie Bungalow
Charlie was called 'bungalow' because he didn't have much upstairs!

Jones Butteraneggs
Jones worked in a grocery shop and whenever anyone made a purchase, he always asked 'butter and eggs?'

Joe Bwgy-bo
Joe the Bogeyman

Ianto Bwtsh and Tom Bwtsh
Both men were butchers.

Owen Jones Caernarfon

Ianto Canary
The minutes of the Miners' Lodge refer to 'Mr E Jones (Canary)'. Ianto was a diminutive form of Evan, who had a fine tenor voice. Ianto would every now and again find everything too much and disappear for a while, taking his chickens with him. There are witnesses who have seen the chickens lying down with their legs in the air waiting to be trussed and carried!

Jimmy Candles
Jimmy had a runny nose (picture an ordinary used candle)!

Shoni Cannon
John Davies was a loud and vocal opponent of Liberal speakers in the local election.

Shoni, Abram and Wil Cardi
They all came from Cardiganshire.

Davies Cardi-bachs
The original 'little Cardis' were short of stature and the family inherited this name.

Evans Cardi Caws
Evans Cardi Cheese

Carno Morgan
Morgan from Carno

Shoni Ceiliog
Johnny Bantam

John Dafis Cerddor
John Dafis Musician

John Check
The 'checker' was a pit-head official.

Jack Thomas Chico
Jack kept chickens.

Ianto Chips

John Rees Cilgerran

Lisa Clocs
Liza Wooden Clogs

Billy and Tom Thomas Cochyn
Both had red or ginger hair.

John Davies and Tom Cockney

Evans y Coesa
Legs Evans

Wil and Dick Come-up

Mari Copa Tin
There is a similar nickname in north Wales which refers to 'a stuck-up backside'!

Mrs Jones Cornerhouse
Mrs Jones of the 'cornerhouse' as opposed to the other Mrs Joneses.

Francis Cos Brwsh
Francis Broom-handle

Dai Crachan
Dai 'Scar'

Ianto Crackshovel

Dick Curalene
Curalene was a home-made ointment *yn gwella popeth ond clefyd y galon* – it cured everything except heartache.

Ianto Cwmaman
Evan from Cwmaman

Glyn Cwmoco
Glyn from Cwm Ogwr (Ogmore Vale)

Evan Cwmpella
Evan from Cwm Pellaf (a place name)

Dai Denbigh

Tommy Devon

Will John Dinger

The Nicknames of Ynys-y bŵl

Dinna Car y Baw
Car y baw was perhaps a 'dram of rubbish'.

Bob Doctor
Bob was well informed on matters medical.

John Dol
John had a wife called Dorothy whom he addressed as 'Dol'.

Morgan Double-power
Morgan Morgans

Dai Dwl
Silly Dai

Ned Dŵr
Ned Water worked in a wet part of the coalface.

John English Cause
John went to an English chapel

Joe Faggots

Will Farmer

Dai Fat

Dic Fawr y Wraig
Big Dick and his wife

Fernato
This formidable mafioso, when young, had difficulty in pronouncing the word 'tomato'.

Dai and John Jones Ffowls
Ffowls (chickens)

Ianto Ffwl Pelt
Ianto Full Pelt (as fast as one can).

Tommy Fossil

Friswith
A feminine name which is not a nickname. There were at least two ladies of this name in the village and, while it is far from being a common name, it does appear frequently enough in various types of parish records to make it notable.

Alby and Arthur Ginger

Ianto Glatsien
Evan 'I'll Give You a Clout' (from *clatsien* 'thump', 'blow' or 'smack').

Jimmy Glory
A dapper little man who attended the Gospel Hall and always carried a Bible.

Ned Glynmynach
Edward from Glynmynach Street

Rhys y Gof
Rhys the Smith

Billy Goodboy
When speaking to any of his fellow miners, Billy referred to them as 'good boy'.

Tommy'r Graig
This nickname comes from a place name.

William Jones Green Peas
William was a greengrocer who called out 'Green peas' on his rounds.

Iesu Grist Bach
Jesus Christ Junior (a very religious man).

Gunner Wall

William Williams Gwallt Gwyn
William Williams White Hair

Shoni Gwladys
John with the formidable Gwladys as his wife.

Evan Gŵr Gwraig
Evan Wife's Husband

Buster Hatch
Buster used to box.

Dick Holyhead

Joe Irish

Dai Jinks
David Jenkins

Jockey Morgan
A diminutive figure

Dai Keeper

Shoni Kill a Pig
Shoni kept pigs and, if he missed work, his excuse was he 'had to kill a pig'.

Joe Lady

John Laga Naw
Laga Naw referred to nine-inch wooden support beams used to shore up the roof underground.

Mrs Davies Lampost
She had a lamppost outside her house which distinguished her from all the other Mrs Davieses in the street.

Gwilym Lampy
He worked in the lamp-room on top pit (the part of the pit above the ground).

Danny Lanky

Tom Lap
He used to have *teisen lap* (a fruit cake) in his tommy (food) box.

John Laplap
John Yackety-yack.

Lisa Lastig
Liza Elastic.

Jack Left
The 'Left' probably referred to his political tendencies.

Tommy Life

Dicky Lightning
He was a ponderous speaker and mover.

The Nicknames of Ynys-y bŵl

Edward Davies Llanidloes

Dai Llaw Bwt
Llaw bwt means 'left-handed', 'southpaw' or 'awkward'.

Tom Llosg
Tom's face had been badly burned in a pit explosion (*llosg* meaning 'burnt').

Lewsin Llygad Lark
Lewis Lark's Eye.

Long Dan

Ianto Lucky

Shoni Machine

Shoni Machynlleth

Wm Evans y Maer
William Evans the Mayor.

Dai Main
Thin Dai.

Twm Mardy
Tom from Maerdy.

Shoni 'Merica
Johnny America.

Dai Minty
He was the owner of a sweet-shop.

David Evans Mochwr
David Evans the Pigman.

Dai Naill Fraich
David Either Arm (ambidextrous).

Jack the Navvy
Jack had worked in the 'Navigation' Colliery.

John No Coal

Billy Nobbs

Billy Nuts
He would say 'I don't want a ton of fruit, only a few nuts.'

Tommy and Billy Onetune
Thomas, the father, played the piano in the silent cinema, playing one tune at different speeds. Billy, the son, didn't but he inherited the 'surname'.

Tom Pembroke
See Tom Pig.

Twm Penlan
Thomas from Penlan.

Shoni Penparc
John from Penparc.

Dai Pepper

Picture Smith

Tom Pig
Tom was a Pembrokeshire Pig (anyone from Pembrokeshire would be called 'pig').

Pennigy Pipe

Plentyn Duw
God's Child.

Dan Pontypridd

Peter Pop
Peter sold pop (fizzy cold drinks) around the streets.

John Pregethwr
John the Preacher.

Tom Jones Prysg
Prysg was the name of a farm in the Rhondda.

Johnny Pups
He bred dogs.

Twm Pwrffelo
Thomas Poor Fellow.

Pwyswr Bach
He was the one who weighed the coal drams (literally 'the little weigher').

Dai Rambler

John Davies Rheumatic

Bob the Runner

Will Salvation
He carried the banner for the Salvation Army.

Roberts Sand y Môr
This was the man who sold sand to the miners' wives (who used it to scour their front doorsteps). Great pride was taken in a terraced row of gleaming doorsteps.

Dick Sara
Richard whose wife's name was Sara.

Dai Sbaddwr
Dai the Castrator.

Sbarcyn Bach yr Uffern
The Little Spark from Hell.

Will Scothwr
Will the Spreader. *Scothi celwydde* in the dialect of Ynys-y-bŵl was 'to spread lies'. *Ysgothi* also means 'to defecate'.

Rachel Scratch

George Shân
George whose wife's name was Shân.

Ben, Dai and Bob Shivone
They were all from Anglesey (from *Sir Fôn* 'Anglesey').

Shoni Siopwr
John the Shopkeeper.

Slasher Hughes

Jimmy Small-coal
Miners were entitled to free coal and, after this was delivered and stored away, there was always a mound of small pieces of coal left, which Jimmy would collect.

The Nicknames of Ynys-y bŵl

Ernie Smiler
He was not a happy soul.

John Snowball

Dai Sospan
He was from Llanelli.

Dai Sporty
Dai was a part-time game-keeper at the Glog country house.

Will Hughes Sound Man

Harry Step-and-Fetch-It

John Sunday Clothes

Arthur Swansea

Jack Sweep
He was a chimney sweep.

Albert Taff
Albert's nickname comes from the River Taff.

Twm Tairhewl
Tairhewl was a local place name.

Dai Teddy Bear

Shoni Teilwr
Johnny the Tailor

Tommy Teisen Wheel
His mother used to ensure he had *teisen wheel* or 'Welsh cakes' in his tommy box.

Ianto the Terror

Ernie Thruppence
This Ernie was the same man as Ernie Smiler

Evan Davies Towyn

Bob Tredegar

Mrs Davies Treorchy

Trigger Hatch

Ted Tuppence

Billy Twicey
William Williams, of course!

Twt Hughes
He was a small man (*twt* meaning 'small' or 'compact').

Evans Tylafarch
His nickname comes from the name of his farm.

Twm Tynewydd
As above, this nickname comes from a farm name.

Dick Whipa Din
Dick I'll Tan your Backside

Dick Whipper-in
Dick was the school attendance officer.

Dai Whistl Dun
Dai Tin Whistle had a voice like a tin whistle.

Wtar Pendarran
The Pendarran Hooter.

Wil y Foelallt
This nickname comes from a place name.

I would like to think that this list of nicknames spans the heyday of the pit and captures something of the spirit of a community and way of life which, like the Lady Windsor Colliery, exists now only in our memories.

The Lady Windsor Colliery, Ynys-y-bŵl, 1884–1988
Jonathan Thomas, carpenter 1875–1957

Girls' Names

A

Adwen
Aelwen
Aeres
Aerona, Aeronwy
Alaw
Alis
Alwen, Alwena
Alys
Aneira
Angharad
Anna
Annest, Anest
Anwen
Arianrhod
Arianwen
Arwen, Arwenna
Aures
Aurona
Awela
Awen, Awena

B

Beca
Begw
Berwen
Bethan
Beti, Betsan
Blodeuwedd
Blodwen
Branwen
Brengain
Briallen
Brianne
Bron
Bronwen
Buddug

C

Cadi
Callwen
Cari
Caronwen
Carrog
Carwen
Caryl
Carys
Cati
Catrin
Ceindeg
Ceinwen
Ceirios
Ceri
Cerian
Ceridwen
Ceris, Cerys
Clwyd
Cothi
Cranogwen
Creiddylad
Creirwy

D

Dafina
Dedwydd
Delwen
Delyth
Derwenna
Deryn
Dilwen
Dilys
Dona
Dwyfor
Dwynwen
Dwyryd
Dwysan
Dwysli
Dyddgu
Dyfi
Dyfyr

E

Ebrill
Efa
Efanna
Eiddwen
Eifiona
Eigr

Girls' Names

Eigra
Eilian
Eilir, Eilyr
Eiluned
Eilwen
Eira
Eirian
Eiriana
Eirianedd
Eirianwen
Eiriol
Eirlys
Eirwen
Eiry
Elain
Elan
Eldryd, Eldrydd
Elen, Elin, Elena
Elenid, Elenydd
Eleri
Elidan
Elin
Elinor
Elliw
Elonwy
Eluned, Luned
Elysteg
Enfys
Enid
Ennis
Erfyl
Erin
Eryl
Eryn
Esyllt
Ethni
Eurddyl
Eurfron
Eurfyl
Eurgain
Euron

Euronwy
Eurwen

F

Faleiry
Fanw
Ffion
Fflur
Ffolant
Ffraid
Fioled

G

Garwen
Gaynor
Generys
Gladys
Glain
Glandeg
Glenda
Glenys
Glesni
Glynis
Goewyn, Goewin
Goleu
Goleuddydd
Golwg Hafddydd
Grug
Gwalia
Gwawr
Gweirfyl
Gwen
Gwenant
Gwenda
Gwenddydd
Gwendolen,
Gwendolyn
Gwendraeth
Gweneth

Gwenfair
Gwenffrwd
Gwenfil
Gwenfrewy,
Gwenffrewi
Gwenfyl
Gwenhwyfar
Gwenith
Gwenllïan
Gwennan
Gwennant
Gwenno
Gwent
Gwenyth
Gwerful, Gwerfyl
Gwladus
Gwladys
Gwlithen
Gwyar
Gwyddfid
Gwylan
Gwyneira
Gwyneth

H

Haf
Hafina
Hafren
Hafwen
Hawen
Hawys
Heddus
Heddwen
Heddys
Hefina
Heledd
Helygen
Heulwen

I

Ifanna
Ilid
Ina
Indeg
Iola
Iona
Irwen

L

Leri
Lili
Lilwen
Lisa
Lleucu
Llewela
Llian
Llinos
Llio
Lluan
Llywela
Lona
Lowri
Luned
Lyn, Lynne
Lynwen

M

Mabli
Madlen
Mai
Mair
Mairwen
Malen
Mali
Mallt
Manod
Manon

Mared
Marged
Margiad
Mari
Marwenna
Mati
Medi
Medwen
Megan
Meinir
Meinwen
Meirwen
Melangell
Meleri
Men
Menai
Menna
Mererid
Merierid
Mirain
Modlen
Moelona
Moelwen
Mona
Morfudd
Morwenna
Myfanwy
Myfi
Myrdeg

N

Nanno
Nerys
Nest
Nesta
Nia
Non
Nona

O

Olwen
Olwenna
Owena

P

Prydwen

R

Rebeca
Rhian
Rhiain
Rhianedd, Rhianydd
Rhiannon
Rhianwen
Rhona
Rhonwen
Rhoswen
Rian
Ronwen

S

Sara
Seren
Shan, Shân, Shani
Siân/Sian
Siani
Sioned
Siriol
Siwan
Sulwen

T

Tanwen
Tathan
Tegau

Girls' Names

Tegwedd
Tegwen
Teleri
Telor
Tonwen, Tonwenna

Trefina
Tudfil, Tudful,
Tudfyl, Tydfil
Tyleri

W

Wenna

Boys' Names

A

Adda
Aelwyn, Aylwyn
Aeron
Aethwy
Afagddu
Afallach
Afan
Afarwy
Alaw
Alban
Alcwyn
Aled
Alun
Alwyn
Amaethon
Amanwy
Amig
Amlyn
Anatiamaros
Andras
Andreas
Aneirin, Aneurin
Anwyl, Annwyl
Arawn
Arfon
Arial
Arnallt
Aron
Arthur
Arwel
Arwyn
Aurfryn
Auryn
Awstin
Aylwyn

B

Baglan
Banadl
Barti
Bedwyr
Bendigeidfran
Berian
Berwyn
Beuno
Bleddyn
Bobi
Bodfan
Bradwen
Braint
Brân
Brenig, Brennig
Brwyn, Brwyno
Brychan
Bryn
Brynach
Brynmor
Brython
Byrnach

C

Cadell
Cadfael
Cadfan
Cadifor, Cydifor
Cadnant
Cadog
Cadwaladr
Cadwallon
Cadwgan
Cadwy
Caeo
Caerwyn
Cai
Caian
Caio
Caledfryn
Camwy
Caradog
Caredig
Caron
Carrog
Carwyn
Casnar
Cedwyn
Cefni
Ceian
Ceidiog
Ceidrych
Ceiriog

Ceiro
Ceitho
Cellan
Celyn
Celynin, Celynen
Cemais
Cennard
Cennydd
Cenwyn
Ceredig
Ceri
Cerian
Ceris, Cerys
Cerith
Cian
Cilmin
Cilydd
Cled
Cledan
Cledlyn
Cledwyn
Clwyd
Clynnog
Collen
Colwyn
Cothi
Creunant
Crwys
Culhwch
Curig
Custennin, Cystennin
Cwyfan
Cybi
Cyfeiliog
Cyffin, Kyffin
Cynan
Cyndeyrn
Cynddylan
Cynddylig
Cynfab
Cynfael, Cynfal

Cynfelin, Cynfelyn
Cynfrig, Cynrig
Cynin
Cynlais
Cynog
Cynon
Cynwal
Cynwyl
Cynyr
Cystennin

D

Dafi
Dafydd
Dai
Dalis
Dathan
Dedwydd
Deganwy
Degwel
Dei
Deian
Deiniol
Delfryn
Delwyn
Derec
Derfel
Deri
Derwen
Derwydd
Derwyn
Deudraeth
Deulwyn
Dewi
Dilwyn
Dinmael
Doiran
Dulais
Dwyfan
Dwyryd

Dyfan
Dyfi
Dyfed
Dyfnallt
Dyfnwal
Dyfri
Dyfrig
Dylan

E

Edern
Edmwnd
Ednyfed
Edryd
Efnysien
Efrog
Egryn
Eic
Eifion
Eilian
Eilir, Eilyr
Eilwyn
Eilyr
Einion
Eirian
Eirig
Eirug
Eirwyn
Eiryl
Eldryd, Eldrydd
Elerydd
Elfed
Elfryn
Elfyn
Elgan
Elgar
Elian
Elidir
Elise
Elvis

Elwyn
Elystan
Emlyn
Emrys
Emyr
Endaf
Eos
Erfyl
Erwyd
Eryl
Eudaf
Eunydd
Eurfryn
Eurfyl
Eurig
Eurof
Euros
Eurwyn
Euryl
Euryn
Eurys

F

Fflamddwyn
Ffolant, Folant
Ffowc
Ffrancon
Floyd
Fychan

G

Galâth
Garan
Gareth
Garin
Garmon
Garnon
Garth
Garwy

Garwyn
Geraint
Gerallt
Gerwyn
Gethin
Gildas
Gilfaethwy
Glandeg
Glanffrwd
Glanmor
Glannant
Glascurion
Glasnant
Gloyw
Glwyddyn
Glyn
Glyndw^r
Glyndwr
Glynog
Gofan
Gomer
Goronw
Goronwy
Gorwel
Griff
Griffith
Griffri
Gronwy
Gronw
Gruff
Gruffudd
Gruffydd
Gurwyn
Guto
Gutyn, Gutun
Gwair, Gweir
Gwalchmai
Gwarnant
Gwawl
Gweirydd
Gwên

Gwenallt
Gwenlyn
Gwenogfryn
Gwent
Gwern
Gwernydd
Gwesyn
Gwidol
Gwili
Gwilym
Gwion
Gwlithyn
Gwri
Gwrtheyrn
Gwyddno
Gwydion
Gwydol
Gwylfa
Gwylon
Gwyn
Gwynallt
Gwynant
Gwyndaf
Gwynedd
Gwynfi
Gwynfil
Gwynfor
Gwynfryn
Gwynn
Gwynno
Gwynoro
Gwyrfai
Gwyrosydd
Gwythyr

H

Hafgan
Hafwyn
Harri, Harry
Hedd

91

Boys' Names

Heddwyn
Hedydd
Hefin
Heilin
Heilyn
Heini
Heulfryn
Heulwyn
Heulyn
Hiraethog
Hiriell
Hobcyn
Howel
Huail
Huw
Hwfa
Hwlcyn
Hyfaidd
Hywel
Hywyn

I

Iago
Ianto
Idloes
Idris
Idwal
Iestyn
Ieuan
Ifan
Ifor
Illtud
Illtyd
Ioan
Iolo
Ion
Iorwerth
Irfon
Irwyn
Isfoel

Isfryn
Islwyn
Ithel
Iwan

K

Keidrych
Kenfyn
Kenwyn
Kyffin

L

Llefelys
Lleu, Llew
Lleufer
Llew
Llewelyn
Llifon
Llion
Lloyd
Lludd
Llwyd
Llŷr
Llywarch
Llywelyn
Luc
Lyn, Lynn

M

Mabon
Machreth
Macsen
Madoc
Madog
Mael
Maelgwn, Maelgwyn
Maelor
Mal

Maldwyn
Manawydan
Manod
Marc
March
Maredudd
Marlais
Marles
Math
Mathonwy
Mechain
Medrod
Medwyn
Mei
Meic
Meidrym
Meilir
Meilyr
Meirion
Meirwyn
Melwas
Merêd
Meredydd
Merfyn
Meriadoc
Mervyn
Meurig
Meuryn
Miall
Mihangel
Milwyn
Moelwyn
Moc
Môn
Mordaf
Morgan
Morien
Morlais
Morris
Morys
Mostyn

Myfyr
Myrddin

N

Nantlais
Nedw
Nefydd
Neifion
Ninian
Now
Nudd
Nye

O

Odwyn
Ogwen
Onllwyn
Oriel
Orig
Orwig
Osian
Oswallt
Owain
Owen

P

Padarn
Pedr
Pedrog
Pennant
Pennar
Penrhyn
Penri
Peredur
Peris
Powys
Pryderi
Prys

Prysor
Pwyll

R

Rheinallt
Rhidian
Rhion
Rhisiart
Rhodri
Rholant
Rhonabwy
Rhosier
Rhoslyn
Rhun
Rhydderch
Rhydian
Rhydwen
Rhys
Rhystud
Rol
Robat
Rolant
Ronw

S

Sandde
Seimon
Seiriol
Seisyll
Selyf
Shon, Shôn, Shoni
Siams
Sianco
Siarl
Sieffre
Siencyn
Silyn
Simwnt
Siôn

Sioni
Sionyn
Siôr
Steffan
Styfin
Sulien
Sulwyn

T

Taffy
Talafan
Talfan
Talfryn
Talhaearn
Talieisin
Taran
Tawe
Tecwyn
Tegerin
Tegid
Tegla
Tegryn
Tegwel
Tegwyn
Teifi
Teifion
Teifryn
Teilo
Telor
Terfel
Terwyn
Tewdwr
Teyrnon
Tomos
Towy
Towyn
Trahaearn
Trebor
Trefin
Trefor

Boys' Names

Tristan
Tryfan
Trystan
Tudfor
Tudno
Tudor
Tudur
Tudwal
T(y)weli
Twm
Twynog
Tydai
Tydfor

Tysul
Tywi
Tywyn

U

Uchdryd
Urien

V

Vaughan

W

Winston
Wyn, Wynn
Wyre

Y

Ynyr
Ywain

Surnames

A

Allet, Allett
Anwyl, Annwyl
Ap Dafydd, ap Gwyn-
    edd, ap Steffan

B

Beddoes
Bellin, Belling
Bellis
Bennion, Benyon,
Bevan
Beynon
Blainey
Blethyn, Blethin,
Blevin, Blythin
Bonner
Bowen
Brace
Brangwyn
Breeze
Brice, Bryce
Brymor
Bumffrey,
Bumphrey
Bunner
Bunnion, Bunyan,
Bunyon

C

Caddick, Caddock
Cadogan
Cadwalader
Cam, Gam, Games
Carn, Carne
Cecil
Cethin
Clough
Cogan
Conway
Cradoc, Craddock
Cule
Cyffin, Kyffin

D

Davy, Davies
Day, Daye
Dee
Devonald
Dewey

E

Edwards
Egham
Einon, Ennion,
Eynon
Elias, Elis, Ellis
Ethall, Ethell
Evans
Eynon

F

Floyd

G

Gam, Games
Gittins, Gittings
Gooch
Gough
Griffin, Griffiths
Gwilliam

H

Harris, Harries,
Harry
Hier
Hopkins
Howell(s)
Hughes, Huws

Surnames

J

Jones

K

Kemys
Kendrick

L

Lewis
Lloyd

M

Mayler
Mayne
Mellen, Mellings
Meredith
Merrick
Meyrick
Morris

N

Nanney

P

Parry
Penry
Povey
Powell
Preece, Price
Prichard, Pritchard
Probert
Prosser
Prothero
Prydderch
Prytherch
Puw, Pughe

R

Rees
Rosser

T

Treharne
Trevor
Tudor

V

Vaughan
Voyle

W

Williams
Winston
Worgan